SPORT PSYCHOLOGY LIBRARY:

TENNIS

SPORT PSYCHOLOGY LIBRARY:

TENNIS

Judy L. Van Raalte
Carrie Silver-Bernstein

Illustrations:
Maribeth Blonski

Fitness Information Technology, Inc.
P.O. Box 4425, University Avenue
Morgantown, WV 26504-4425 USA

Illustration Credit: Drawings are by Maribeth Blonski

Library of Congress Card Catalog Number: 98-73846

ISBN 1-885693-16-8

Copyeditor: Sandra R. Woods
Cover Design: James R. Bucheimer
Developmental Editor: Geoffrey C. Fuller
Production Editor: Craig R. Hines
Printed by: Data Reproductions Corporation

Printed in the United States of America
10   9   8   7   6   5   4   3   2   1

Fitness Information Technology, Inc.
P.O. Box 4425, University Avenue
Morgantown, WV 26504 USA
(800) 477-4348
(304) 599-3482
Email: fit@fitinfotech.com
Web Site: www.fitinfotech.com

About the Sport Psychology Library

With this book I am pleased to introduce the Sport Psychology Library, a unique contribution to the sports world. For the first time ever, sport psychologists, coaches, and athletes have combined their skills and experiences to bring you a series of books that show athletes, coaches, and parents how to achieve maximum benefits from their sports involvement. Each book in the series is focused on a specific sport, so your special needs as a participant in that sport will be directly addressed. I am delighted that the first book in the series is by two remarkable professionals, sport psychologist Judy Van Raalte and tennis coach Carrie Silver-Bernstein. As a tennis player myself, I know how useful this book will be for all readers.

As Editor-in-Chief of the Sport Psychology Library, I have the privilege of reviewing each book in the library. The result is that while each book in the series stands alone and deals with the factors unique to that sport, the books combine to build an outstanding library of knowledge about the psychology of sport. Expect us to provide about 2–3 books for the Library each year.

Now, it's time for me to get out of the way so that you can proceed with the job of becoming a better tennis player! Enjoy!

Shane Murphy, Ph.D.
Editor-in-Chief
Sport Psychology Library

Dr. Shane Murphy is the former head of the Sport Psychology Department of the United States Olympic Committee and is currently President of Gold Medal Psychological Consultants.

About the Authors

Judy L. Van Raalte, Ph.D., is an Associate Professor of Psychology at Springfield College in Springfield, Massachusetts, a member of the US Olympic Committee Registry of sport psychologists, and a Certified Sport Psychology Consultant, Association for the Advancement of Applied Sport Psychology. She has provided sport psychology services to NCAA Division I, II, and III tennis teams as well as a number of competitive junior tennis players. Judy is also an avid tennis player. Currently, she is ranked #5 in New England in the Open division. Her strokes aren't always pretty, but she is mentally tough! In her years as a college coach she acquired a 51–12 win loss record for a .81 winning percentage.

Carrie Silver-Bernstein is the head tennis coach at University of Hartford, an NCAA Division I institution. She has been coaching at the college and high school levels for 8 years, acquiring an 86–25 win–loss record. A licensed physical therapist and certified athletic trainer, Carrie is a co-chair of the National Strength and Conditioning Association Special Interest Group for Tennis. She is also president of Team Conditioning Concepts, a company that provides comprehensive fitness, health, and psychological skills training for competitive tennis players and other athletes. Carrie is a skilled athlete. Since 1997 she was ranked #1 in Open Division doubles in New England (with coauthor Van Raalte) and played on the East region soccer team that won the Nutmeg Games.

Table of Contents

Acknowledgments

Much of the inspiration for this book has come from the outstanding coaches and players with whom we have been privileged to work. Special thanks to coaches Judy Dixon, Edsel Ford, Dan Gimble, Sheila MacInerney, and Helen Palmer; assistant coaches Linda Barton, Debbie Blocker Merwitz, Peter Bradshaw, Ludi Cosio-Lima, Jennifer Di Prete, Marc Gerstein, Denise Lintel, Jessica Sullivan; and the tennis teams of Springfield College, Tufts University, University of Connecticut, University of Hartford, and E. O. Smith High School.

We received excellent editorial assistance from the staff at FIT, Shane Murphy, Andy Ostrow, and Sandra Woods. Thanks also to our anonymous reviewers as well as to Janet Freundlich, Steve Klopfer, Margy Leinhardt, Sandy and Bob Silver, Jane Taylor, and Marilyn and Peter Van Raalte.

Finally we would like to give special thanks to Rick Bernstein, Britt Brewer, and Hayden and Travis Van Brewer for their support on this project. We could not have done it without them.

Support for this project was provided by Springfield College for sabbatical leave for Judy L. Van Raalte.

Illustrator

Maribeth Blonski is a children's book illustrator, multimedia/fine artist, and educational software specialist. She holds a Bachelor of Fine Arts from the Hartford Art School at the University of Hartford in West Hartford, Connecticut. Extensive work and studies in Europe give her illustrations a uniquely varied dimension. Maribeth is the illustrator of *The Story of the Christmas Bear, Queen of the Kisses, Queen of the Kisses Meets Sam Under a Soup Pot, Long Term Care Nursing Standards, Policies, & Procedures,* and *The Caterpillar Had a Dream.*

Tips to Improve Your Game

1

INTRODUCTION

Tennis is a game for life. You can play it at many levels. You can improve at any stage. We wrote this book for people who want to play better tennis.

Purpose of the Book

When you have a tennis problem, you look for a tennis solution. You want immediate help. In this book we show you how to improve your mental and emotional game. Here's how it works. Each chapter deals with a specific tennis issue. Read the chapter about your problem and you will find several ways to improve your game. You may gain extra insight into your problem from answering the "think about your game" questions (see *Style of Play* on the next page). You will also want to try the on-court exercises, both mental and physical, designed to help you improve specific aspects of your

STYLE OF PLAY

Circle the answer that best describes you.

1. My favorite shots to hit are
    a. ground strokes from the baseline.
    b. angle shots from the baseline.
    c. both ground strokes and volleys.
    d. volleys.

2. In pressure situations,
    a. I stay consistent and wait for my opponent to make an error.
    b. I am consistent, but go for winners when I get a short ball.
    c. I hit ground strokes or come to the net, whatever is needed.
    d. I serve and volley.

3. I usually win points by
    a. outlasting my opponents.
    b hitting aggressive ground stroke winners.
    c. coming to the net on short balls and volleying.
    d serving aces or serving and volleying.

4. My movement around the court is
    a. usually from *behind* the baseline, side to side.
    b. usually *on* the baseline, side to side.
    c. usually both side to side and forward to the net.
    d. usually from the baseline forward to the net.

5. My mental game plan usually is
    a. to wear my opponent down.
    b. to attack the ball from the baseline.
    c. to attack from wherever in the court I can.
    d. to put the ball away as quickly and aggressively as possible.

If the majority of your answers are "a," you are a classic baseline player; "b," you are an aggressive baseline player; "c," you are an all-court player; "d," you are a serve-and-volleyer. Each type of player has strengths and weaknesses (see *How to Beat Almost Anyone* on page 4). Enhancing your strengths and improving your weaknesses will bring out the best in your game.

game. If you have more than one problem, read more than one chapter. It's that simple.

The second purpose of this book is to encourage you to use your (sometimes hidden) strengths. You will notice as you read that we present a number of ideas to help you improve your game. Having several options to deal with a situation enables you to select the best approach for you. Your approach may not work for your doubles partner, but it could be your saving grace. If it works for you, we want you to use it! Go with what works.

On some days even your saving grace can't help your game. This book has suggestions for those days, too. If the best solution (Plan A) isn't working, there are tips so you can go to Plan B or even Plan C.

What Is in the Book

The book is organized into six sections: beating the players you hate to play, dealing with pressure, handling the things that you can't control, enjoying doubles, managing when your game falls apart, and getting (and staying) in the game. Crucial mental skills, such as building confidence, managing anxiety, concentrating, improving focus, staying positive, and increasing motivation, are described. Specific exercises that can be used to develop your mental skills are presented throughout the book. The advantage of this book (compared to other sport psychology books) is that the mental and physical skills needed to handle challenging tennis situations are presented *together*. Thus, you will obtain the combined benefit of practicing specific psychological and technical tennis techniques you need to enhance your game. Each section is described in more detail below.

Beating the players you hate to play. You are bound to be nervous when you find out that you have to play one of those players who drives you crazy. Your nightmare could be the really steady players who seem to hit back everything. If so, chapter 2, "Facing Retrievers," will provide some good advice. Maybe you find the aggressive power hitter most challenging. In that case, see chapter 3, "Playing the Club Champion," and find out how to manage the pressure and pace.

HOW TO BEAT ALMOST ANYONE

Type of Player	Strength	How to build on your strength	Weakness	How to improve your weakness	How to Win
Baseliner	steady	*25-Ball Drill* on on page 13—consistency drill	trouble with short balls	*Fire It Up!* drill on page 29	Make opponent move forward and back in the court; vary patterns; attack short balls.
Aggressive Baseliner	aggressive	*Fire It Up!* on page 29—aggressive drill	trouble with "junk" balls	*Consistency drill* on page 15	Change the pace; alternate between soft balls and power shots; hit high, deep, bouncing balls.
All-Court Player	hits variety of shots well	*Fire It Up!* on page 29—aggressive drill	trouble choosing what shot to hit	*Strategy Drill* on page 67—strategy drill	Hit to opponent's weakness; hit deep shots.
Serve-and-Volleyer	strong serve	*Crosscourt Consistency Drill* on page 93—come to net on Volleyer	inconsistent ground strokes, lack of patience	25 Ball Drill on page 13—ground stroke drill	Capitalize on opponent's second serve; focus on (and win) your own service game.

Oh the pressure! This section is about dealing with tennis pressure in its many forms. Chapter 4 describes how to handle the high floaters, soft and spin serves, and other dreaded easy shots that leave so many players yelling, "How could I have missed that?" Chapter 5 covers the big points that make some players furious when they whack the ball out or dink it into the net. It is not just individual points that carry pressure. Chapter 6 has suggestions that will have you playing your best in the big matches.

What to do about those nasty things you can't control. You can work on your tennis game and really improve, but there are some aspects of tennis that you just can't control. No matter who you are, there are some challenges that you have to deal with. In chapter 7, suggestions are made to help handle the vagaries of the tennis environment, everything from poor lighting to snowy roads en route to matches. Unfortunately, Mother Nature is not the only uncontrollable adversary you will face on the courts. You may run into opponents who make questionable line calls or who bring cheering sections to your matches. Chapter 8 discusses ways to overcome human challenges.

Delights and dreads of doubles. Playing doubles well requires additional mental skills. Chapter 9 describes the important steps that you can take to ensure that you are part of a great team. In some cases, you will find that your doubles partner is not a very good player. Chapter 10 has suggestions for playing your best when you can't count on your partner's game. Sometimes it is not your partner who is out to lunch, it is you. Chapter 11 will give you some tips for dealing with the game when you let your partner down.

What to do if it all falls apart. This is the emergency section of the book. If your tennis problems are overwhelming, then this section is for you. Chapter 12 will help you recover your tennis strokes. Chapter 13 will put your mental game back on track. After reading these two chapters you will find yourself playing better quickly.

Getting (and staying) in the game. If you have someone in your life (a friend, a child, a spouse) who wants to become involved in tennis, then turn to chapter 14. Everything from what equipment to buy to when to start playing is discussed here. Maybe you've played tennis for a while, but have been forced out due to injuries. Chapter 15 describes methods for getting into top tennis condition and also has some suggestions for the best ways to recover from common tennis injuries.

What You Will Learn From This Book

This book is designed to help you get the most out of your game. You do this by identifying your talents and using them. Taking advantage of your best skills is exactly what a good coach would have you do. This book teaches you to "be your own coach."

This book will also help you direct your practice sessions. By thinking critically about your game, you will identify what aspects of your game you need to work on. You will then have specific tennis drills and mental skills techniques to practice.

When you use this book, you may find that an idea that made sense to you when reading didn't work on the first try. That's OK. Keep practicing. Mental skills are like physical skills, they take some time to develop. If you read a chapter and try only one of the many suggestions, that's fine. Use what works for you now. If you reread chapters periodically, you will find that you can continually reenergize your game.

Summary

Playing better tennis is not all that hard to do. It takes a combination of physical practice and mental training. Take some time to "think about your game" and answer the questions presented in the book. Use the drills and exercises to enhance your strengths and overcome your weaknesses. With some self-assessment and on-court practice you will find that your tennis game can be more consistent, more aggressive, more confident, more focused, more positive, and more fun.

BEATING THE PLAYERS YOU HATE TO PLAY

(OH NO! MY OPPONENT IS A _____)

2

FACING RETRIEVERS

Which players present the toughest mental challenge? Not the really big hitters, no! It is the opponents who hit strange spins or high lobs, or who push back those soft shots that drive you crazy. You start off expecting an easy victory. But in the warm-up, their weird game makes it hard for you to find a groove or feel your rhythm. Often, you start out winning but they get a racquet on a lot of balls. They may hit lucky winners, frame shots, or those that skim the net and dribble annoyingly over onto your side. They may even win a game. Then it turns out to be two games, and you start to try to hit bigger shots, or you hold back so you don't hit out, and now you're frustrated. That is why retrievers are the worst kind of players to play.

Not all retrievers hit with funny spins or get all the lucky shots. What retrievers do have in common is mental toughness. If you find yourself having trouble playing a retriever (sometimes called hackers, lobbers, or pushers), never fear. There are several things you can try to do to improve your chances. On the other hand, if you are a retriever yourself, keep reading closely for some good ideas on how to be an even tougher opponent!

Retrievers Are Hard to Beat

Sure, you don't expect to win every match you play. You don't mind losing (that much) to people who can really hit the ball. Sometimes when you lose to someone great, you can walk off the court feeling good about your game. When you play a retriever, however, you often leave the court feeling frustrated even if you are the winner. There are several reasons why.

They Make You Overconfident

When you warm up with a retriever, you may be psyched about the match. Retrievers usually don't have much power or pace. Sometimes these players don't even look like athletes. Your good shots may literally blow them off the court. Of course, you may not get that much of an actual warm-up because they hit off-paced balls and spend a lot of time saying "oops." You don't mind because it seems as if it will be an easy match. You are overconfident.

They Make You Overhit

As the match proceeds, you may grow tired of the soft shots. This may be a worse problem when you have people watching you play. You want to look like the player that you know you are, not some hacker. So, you try to generate more power. The softer your opponent hits, the harder you hit. Unfortunately, your balls start going out more. You are overhitting.

They Make You Tentative

So you find you can't beat the retriever easily. You take a few breaths. You try to calm down. You are going to keep control. You are not going to overhit anymore. You try anything you can to keep the ball in. You become nervous and tight and start to lose your confidence (see *Four Quick Ways to Build Your Confidence* on page 14). You can't make your body do what you want. You have resorted to playing the retriever's game and you are missing more than ever. Arrgggh!

They Make You Frustrated

You are out there trying to play. Your opponent is not hitting any clear winners. The problem is you. You're beating yourself. You are trying anything and everything but nothing is working. You are more and more frustrated (see *Consistency Drill* on page 15 for ways to decrease your frustration and improve your mental endurance).

They Mess Up Your Focus

The ball seems to be right there for you to hit. You have all the time in the world. Instead of just stepping in and hitting it, you start thinking . . . Should I hit it crosscourt or maybe just try anything to get it back? My backhand is off today. I have to win this point! With your racing thoughts the retriever has gotten to you, and you can't focus the way you should.

Solutions

Kathy S. was a solid college athlete who hated playing tennis tournaments in the summer because she would often end up playing retrievers. As her matches progressed, Kathy would start slamming her shots, often right at her opponent. Of course, Kathy's game would fall apart. Kathy became visibly upset at having to play people who "couldn't play the real game."

The solution to Kathy's problem was relatively straightforward. It can work for you, too. Be patient, use your strengths, stay calm, and be positive. Soon, you will find that you can give retrievers a run for their money.

Be Patient

When you play a retriever, it is probably going to be frustrating. You will need to be extra patient with yourself when you miss an easy shot. Everyone misses some easy shots in these sorts of matches. The best players are prepared for it; they recover from their mistakes and stay patient.

One way to be more patient is to think of the points as a drill. You might try to develop different patterns. For example, try hitting with consistency and aim to hit 4 (or even 10) balls over the net in a row. You might try to hit one shot deep to the forehand side, then one short and wide to the backhand side. Hitting in patterns will help you to focus on the ball, find your rhythm, and take your mind off your frustration with your opponent.

It will be easier for you to be patient if you are getting to most of the balls in the match. With a retriever, however, you may find yourself lunging for a lot of soft balls at the last minute. If you are constantly running forward during the points, make it easier on yourself. Take a few steps in and play from this spot. We know that this is the "no man's (nowhere) land" that you have been warned to avoid. Although you usually do not want to be playing from here, having a head start on short balls (and returns of weak serves) will help your consistency against a retriever.

Remember, retrievers hit back a lot of balls (see *25-Ball Drill* on the next page to prepare yourself for a long match). Get yourself into position, be prepared, and stay patient. Be mentally in the match and do what it takes to win.

Use Your Strengths

Playing retrievers can cause you to lose confidence in your regular game plan. News flash—they are grand masters at the retriever game and will probably beat you at it if you decide to try to play it. What you need to do is to stick with your

25-BALL DRILL

Skill objective: Improve your consistency
Psychological objective: Stay confident in long points

Procedure
1. Stand at the baseline.
2. Have a partner feed you 25 balls, alternating one to the forehand side and one to the backhand side.
3. Have the feeder vary the difficulty of the shots.
4. Hit as many balls as you can over the net and in the court.
5. Keep track of the number of balls you hit in a row and try to improve on your record.

Options
1. Try to return all balls crosscourt.
2. Try to return all balls down-the-line.
3. Have your partner feed you 25 balls anywhere in the court.

strengths, but modify them for this type of match. If you are a baseliner, you may have to hit a few more balls than usual before you can hit a good angle shot. You should still go for your good angles, but wait until you have an opening. If you are a net player, come in and volley. If your opponent throws up a lot of lobs, stick with your main plan but modify it slightly. When you come to the net, hang back a few steps. You will find that you can reach those overheads and put them away. Retrievers often hit soft returns that give you the advantage at the net. If you come in, you may be able to end a point and your misery more quickly.

Stay Calm

Retrievers know that they are retrievers. They stick with their game plan throughout the match. They don't get too high or too low emotionally after any particular point. This is one of the things that makes them so hard to play against. If you see yourself getting frustrated when you are playing a retriever, realize that your opponent can probably sense it or see it too. The frustration reaction is exactly what a retriever is hoping

FOUR QUICK WAYS TO BUILD CONFIDENCE

1. Focus on tennis success.
   — Recall a well-hit forehand.
   — Recall winning a match.
   — Recall a great serve.
2. Think positively.
   — Are you thinking negative thoughts?
   — Identify an aspect of your game that is working well now (e.g., trying hard, good forehand, movement).
   — Identify an aspect of your game you will work on next time you play (you no longer have to worry about it today).
3. Put yourself in the "now."
   — Forget the past, the score, your last shot.
   — Focus on the current point, the here, the now.
   — Know you can do it, one point at a time.
4. Use a mental anthem.
   — Think of a confidence-building theme song.
   — Play the song in your mind and use the music's energy.

for. Regain your composure, keep playing, you will take away your opponent's biggest weapon: your self-destruction.

Use Positive Self-Talk

If playing retrievers makes you miserable, then you will need extra moral support to get you through. Be your own cheering section. Banish the "I should have already won," "I can't believe I blew that easy shot," "Nothing is feeling right" dialogue from your on-court vocabulary. Especially when you are playing retrievers, you need to reinforce your effort. Be positive about trying to make your opponent run or come to the net. Stay positive even if you don't win the point every time. Try saying or thinking "good job," "way to get them running," or "keep it up" to help yourself stay in the match.

CONSISTENCY DRILL

Skill objective: Improve ball placement
Psychological objective: Enhance mental endurance for long points

Procedure
1. Play a set with a practice partner.
2. Move your opponent around the court; do not hit power "winners."
3. Give yourself the point if your opponent can't get to the ball (e.g., a drop shot) or if your opponent misses the ball (hits it out or into the net).

Options
1. You lose the point if you hit a clear winner.
2. You can hit a power shot only off a short ball that bounces inside the service line (this helps you combine aggressive play with patience).

Tips
1. Use a full follow-through to reduce errors.
2. Maintain good footwork.
3. Relax—it often takes a few games to get the rhythm of this drill.

Although this self-talk can seem silly, it is really important and helpful. Research shows that the less negative you are, the more likely you are to win. To put it another way, usually a match is one against one. When you are negative, it becomes two (your opponent and your negativity) against one (you).

Summary

Playing retrievers can test your tennis will. These types of matches can make you so frustrated that you overhit, lose confidence, or lose focus. When you know what to do, however, you can rise to the challenge. Be patient, use your strengths, and be positive! If you do, you will find that when you play a retriever, you are the one who wins.

3

PLAYING THE CLUB CHAMPION

You are playing in a tennis tournament so you go to check the draw to see who your opponent will be. You're excited about playing in the tournament and a little nervous. Then you see the draw. You feel yourself start to sweat. You are the one who has to play the club champion (or the first seed, a ranked player, someone who always beats you). "Why me?" you think, and you notice this sinking feeling in your stomach.

If you recognize that sinking feeling or are even feeling it right now just reading this scenario, read the rest of this chapter. If you do, you will learn that playing the club champion (or any other great player) can be a challenge, but it is not as bad as you think because you can overcome your nervousness, you can prepare for the match, you can try new things, and you might even win! Take the quiz in *Playing Under Pressure* below to learn more about how you respond to playing under pressure.

You Can Overcome Your Nervousness

Playing the club champion brings out all of your insecurities. You may feel extra pressure because you don't want to embarrass yourself on the court. You may be worried about other people watching your match. You have the added burden of playing the "top gun," which can cause you to build up your opponent's game in your mind. We admit that there are reasons that you might feel nervous.

PLAYING UNDER PRESSURE

Playing a really good opponent can be rough. It tests both your physical skills and your mental toughness. How do you respond to this type of match?

1. Are you focused and ready to play when the match starts?

    ready   1   2   3   4   5   6   7   not ready

2. Are you mentally in the game?

    ideal focus   1   2   3   4   5   6   7   distracted

3. How do your muscles feel?

    relaxed   1   2   3   4   5   6   7   tense

4. Do you lose your concentration during the match?

    almost never   1   2   3   4   5   6   7   often

Add the numbers you have circled above. If your total is less than 16, you are prepared for most of your big matches. If your total is 16 or greater, you probably do not play as well as you could in pressure situations. Pay special attention to this chapter. Deep, slow breathing (see page 19) is an important tool to prepare you for competition.

DEEP, SLOW BREATHING

1. Breathe deeply from your stomach (make your stomach go in and out, keep your shoulders down).
2. Breathe in for a slow count of three; exhale for a slow count of six.
3. Repeat 2–3 times (or as many times as you need).
4. If you are on the court, refocus on tennis. Tell yourself, "I am ready. I feel good."

The club champion is easier to play than you think because there is absolutely no pressure on you. You are the underdog. You are not expected to win. If you lose every single point in the entire match, it won't matter because you are not expected to win. Enjoy the situation where the pressure is on the other person. Less pressure can help you to be more relaxed and can get your strokes flowing. This can only happen, however, if you let go of your insecurities and focus on your play.

It is hard to relax if you keep thinking that you are going to lose the match, the whole match. When you play the club champion, it is doubly important to play one point at a time. After all, you have to win points before you win games. Once you win games, then you can think about winning sets; and only after you win sets should you think about winning the match. If you focus on your strategy and on hitting the ball, you will find that you are too busy playing tennis to be nervous.

You Can Prepare for the Match

One of the reasons that good players are intimidating is that they *are* good. If you dwell on how good your opponent is, it will affect how you play even when your opponent is having an off day. The highly ranked player has won many matches. The highly ranked player has not won every match. Don't assume that your opponent will win before you start. Come prepared to play, both psychologically and physically.

After all, it can be your *expectations* of your opponent that affect how you play. Shane S. competed in his state high school tennis championships as a sophomore. The championships were held at a big stadium where top pros regularly competed. Shane was understandably nervous. When it was time for his match, Shane walked out on the court with his trusty old racquet. His opponent appeared out of nowhere, dressed in perfect tennis whites and carrying *three* racquets, all brand new. During the warm-up, Shane thought to himself, "What an honor to be playing such a fine athlete." Of course when the match started, Shane didn't stand a chance. He was down 0–6, 0–3 before he noticed that his opponent had no passing shot on his backhand side. If Shane just hit the ball deep to the backhand and came in, he won the point every time. Sadly, this realization came too late. Shane lost the match 0–6, 4–6. Basically, Shane didn't lose to a great player; he lost to the image of a great player that he had built up in his mind.

To prepare psychologically for a big match, relax and remind yourself that playing this competitor is an opportunity for you to improve your game. To enhance your mental preparation, scout your opponent (see chapter 6 for more about scouting). This will help you know whether you have to get ready for a power hitter, a serve-and-volleyer, a killer forehand hitter, or a lefty slicer. Knowing what to expect before the match starts can help you to keep things in perspective.

When you find out what kind of player the club champion is, you can start your physical preparation for the match. If your opponent is a big hitter, try to fit some practice time in with someone who hits hard. If that is not possible, try watching some of the pros play on TV. Just watching the rhythm of their rallies will help you get used to the faster tempo. Besides, you may pick something up watching them. It couldn't hurt, right? If the club champ hits slice or heavy topspin, try to hit with someone who can give you the chance to practice those shots. Also prepare to deal with the champion's strengths by developing a counter plan. Big topspin players generally hate low balls, so work on hitting low balls. The idea is to prepare to play the way you will need to play in your match.

HANDLE THE PRESSURE

Skill objective: Improve play in pressure situations
Psychological objective: Stay relaxed and focused

Procedure
1. Play a set with a practice partner.
2. Modify the scoring so that the player who reaches "30" first wins the game. Games are a maximum of 3 points.

Options
1. Use one serve only (no second serve).
2. Start the set score at 3–3.

Tips
1. Use relaxation techniques (*Big Points Made Easy in Four Steps* on page 39) to help decrease pressure.
2. Practicing in pressure situations will help you perform better in a match.

You Can Try New Things

When you play the club champion, some of your usual shots can land you in big trouble. Maybe you hit a soft return of serve that usually throws people off, but your opponent is smacking it for a winner every time. Never fear, just modify. Remember that you have nothing to lose. You can try out a new strategy and see how it works. You may want to use your opponent's power to give your shots more heat. You'll have to get your racquet back early and make sure to step into the ball to handle this sort of play. You may want to try rushing the net. Sure, your opponent may pass you, but you may also find that you are volleying well. It can be easier to hit good volleys off solid shots than off floating sitters. Remember, if your game is not working, trying new things can be fun. Practicing new skills will pay off in improved play in your next matches, too.

If your opponent is a power hitter, you may want to try hitting mixed-pace balls and lobs. Power hitters often practice with other power hitters. Hitting some off-pace balls may surprise them and take them out of their usual rhythm.

You may want to try to be extra steady, to return a lot of balls. A player who is used to winning probably wants to get off the court quickly. The longer you can make the match, the more frustrated your opponent is likely to become. Your opponent may even start overhitting and missing shots. It could happen.

You Can Win the Match

If you start winning against a top-notch player, then you are in a nice position. Many strong players are not used to losing, so they become frustrated or distracted. If this happens, keep playing hard. Don't start daydreaming about how great it will be when the match is over and about where you will put the trophy. Daydreaming takes your mind off the here and now. Keep your eye on the ball, and play each individual point.

Play each individual point! We cannot stress this idea strongly enough. Play one point at a time, and you will play better tennis even when you are ahead in the match. Playing well when you're ahead can be a challenge. Carolyn H. was given a 5-F-2 trophy at the end of the season. The 5-F-2 was for when she was ahead 5–2 in matches but then would think about winning and how there was only one more game in the set and it was so close and suddenly it seemed, the score would be 5–5. You can guess what the F on the trophy stood for! It is hard to play well when you are ahead in a match because you start thinking about winning and lots of other things. We think that the F on the 5-F-2 trophy should also stand for Focus (see *Handle the Pressure* for some on–court drills to improve your focus). When you are ahead in a match, keep playing each individual point and keep your focus.

Remember, although you are winning, you were not "supposed to" win. Enjoy where you are and try to keep playing the way you have been playing. If you keep your mind on the points, the match will take care of itself.

You Can Have Fun

Sometimes when you play a strong opponent, you know that you are not going to win many points. That's not the end of the world. It's a character builder. Actually, a game builder. Learn from the situation what your strengths and weaknesses are and what you want to improve for the future. Remember, when the match is over, you can tell your tennis friends what it was like when you played the club champion and survived.

Summary

Playing challenging matches is part of tennis. Take advantage of the opportunity to play someone better than you by overcoming your nervousness, preparing for the match, and trying something new. If you do, you will find that you are a winner, no matter what the score is.

OH THE PRESSURE!

SECTION II

4

THE DREADED EASY SHOTS

You're out there hitting, running, and giving your best when finally the easy one comes your way. It could be a weak second serve, a short lob, a drop shot that doesn't drop, or a floating volley. You get a big grin on your face, smack the ball, and can't believe when it goes into the bottom of the net or the back fence. "Arrggggh! How could I have missed that one?!"

A soft ball often comes as a welcome surprise. Many players find, however, that "easy" shots are also a challenge. If you find yourself missing some balls you expect to put away, don't worry. There are ways to take advantage of these easy shots. Although easy shots are not always that simple, you will hit easy shots better if you work on your tennis technique and develop your mental skills (see quiz in *Your Mental Game* to assess your mental game).

YOUR MENTAL GAME

What kind of player are you? How do you respond to the pressure of competition?

1. How do you feel about competing?
    a. I thrive on pressure.
    b. I like to play matches.
    c. I get nervous playing matches.
    d. I like to practice, not compete.

2. When the pressure is on, do you
    a. try to ace your opponent?
    b. go for winners?
    c. play steady?
    d. hit defensive lobs?

3. If a soft, short ball comes to you, where do you hit it?
    a. Anywhere, as hard as I can.
    b. A power approach shot.
    c. To my opponent's backhand (or other weakness).
    d. A short ball back over.

4. What is your typical outcome after hitting a short ball?
    a. I hit a winner.
    b. I hit it hard, but it went out.
    c. I hit it too soft.
    d. I hit it over, and play continued.

5. How do you respond emotionally if you miss an easy ball?
    a. Mad. I hate it when I miss those.
    b. Fired up. I plan to smash the next easy ball.
    c. I don't worry. It's just one point.
    d. Calm. I prepare for the next ball.

If the majority of your answers are "a" or "b," see *Target Practice* on the next page for a drill to help you with consistency and control. If you answered the majority of the questions "c" or "d," see *Fire It Up!* (also next page) for a drill that will help you be more aggressive.

TARGET PRACTICE

Skill objective: Improve your control
Psychological objective: Stay focused

Procedure
1. Place targets (e.g., tennis ball can, cone) in the back court, three feet inside the intersection of the baseline and sideline.
2. Have a partner feed you soft balls that bounce in the service box.
3. Hit the ball down the line at the target.
4. Work on placement and consistency, not power.
5. Hit as many balls in a row as you can without missing.

Options
1. Practice this with your forehand and backhand.
2. Move the target four feet in front of the service line and two feet from the alley. Hit the ball crosscourt at the target.

Tips
1. Think calming key words before you hit to help you focus (e.g., smooth, easy —see *Key Words* on page 37 for more key words).
2. If you become frustrated, use relaxation techniques (see *Deep, Slow Breathing* on page 19).

FIRE IT UP!

Skill objective: Attack short balls
Psychological objective: Be aggressive

Procedure
1. Place targets (e.g., tennis ball can, cone) near the service line (three feet in from the alley and four feet behind the service line).
2. Have a partner feed you soft balls that bounce in the service box.
3. Hit the ball hard and deep *past* the target toward the back corners of the court (make sure to use a full follow-through).

Options
1. Practice this with your forehand and backhand.
2. Move the target back and work on increasing depth and power.

Tips
1. Use energizing key words before you hit (e.g., attack, power! see *Key Words* on page 37 for more key words).
2. Keep working on hitting aggressively even though balls go out. You will gain more consistency with practice.

Technique

Many players find that some simple physical adjustments can help them to take advantage of easy shots. Practice using good footwork, hitting the ball on the rise or at the top of the bounce, and following through. If you do, you will find these are your favorite shots to hit.

Footwork. If you hit easy shots out, you may think that it is because you are overswinging. The problem is probably not your swing at all, it's your feet. That's right, your feet. You miss easy shots when you don't move your feet enough to be set up for shots hit right to you or when you try to time the easy shot perfectly.

A shot hit right to you is nice, especially if you have been doing a lot of running in the match. No matter how close the shot is to you, though, you still have to be in proper position to hit. Therein lies the footwork problem. If you catch your breath and mentally relax instead of getting set to hit, you are heading for an easy-shot mistake. Keep your feet moving even when you don't have to run for a ball, and you will overcome one of the easy shot demons.

Sometimes the dreaded easy shot is not hit right to you. If the soft, easy ball comes as a serve or a shot hit short in the court, you have to run to the ball. One of the reasons people miss these easy shots is that they try to time things to get to the ball at the exact moment to hit. On soft balls, that means actually waiting before running for the ball or running more slowly than usual. In this situation if you are late even a fraction of a second, then you are in trouble and out of position. You'll have to sprint, lunge, or dive to reach the ball, which has probably dropped below the height of the net, and you'll have to hit up on it so it clears the net. These balls tend to fly out of the court. In hitting great tennis shots, as in life, timing is everything.

To solve the easy-shot timing challenge, move your feet, step up, and hit the ball early. When the short ball comes your way, sprint to it as fast as you can. If you have to wait for a high ball to come down, use little steps to make last-second adjustments to settle into hitting position. When you get to the ball early, it is easy to make minor adjustments for the wind, an odd bounce, or spin. Basically, get to soft balls early and hit them at the top of the bounce, above the height of the net, and you are on your way to easy-shot victory.

The swing. OK, moving your feet and hitting the ball on the rise is a good plan, but what if you don't get to the ball in time? No matter how motivated you are, an easy shot can sometimes take you by surprise. Letting the ball drop below the height of the net requires you to modify your high power swing to keep the ball in the court.

If you change your swing for an easy shot, don't go overboard. You will probably have good results if you shorten your backswing and use your regular, full follow-through. Shortening your backswing allows you to make contact with the ball sooner. Hitting through the ball gives it extra topspin, which will keep it in the court. Don't go for the glory shot on this one. Keep the ball in play. Hit gloriously next time, when you are in position and can catch the ball at the top of the bounce.

Practice. How do you learn to modify your swing to handle these welcome easy shots? Actually, you do it the same way that you train your feet to get you to the ball to hit early. You practice it. Funny, people spend lots of time practicing their ground strokes. They take buckets of balls out to practice serves, but you almost never see people practice hitting easy shots. It is no wonder that these shots are missed so often. Practice going for winners on the easy shot (see *Fire It Up!*), but also practice hitting for consistency (see *Target Practice*) when you are not quite in position.

If you have trouble on easy shots, you know that it is not just the physical challenges that make them difficult, it is the mental challenge. Part of the reason these are called "dreaded easy shots" is that they seem like "gimmes" when they are coming over the net. You may be so sure that you are going to hit a winner off a gimme that you choke and miss the shot. To be mentally strong you should stay focused, have a plan, use finesse, and stay in the match.

Psychological

When a soft ball comes your way, rise to the challenge. Don't mentally mess yourself up. By calling these balls easy shots, you are making things hard on yourself. When you think of the shots this way, you don't give yourself the credit you deserve if you hit the ball well. After all, it was so easy. If you make an error, then you get mad because you can't believe you missed. Either way you mentally lose. What you should do to solve this problem is redefine the situation. Think of these as regular shots or even as "dreaded easy shots." A dreaded easy shot requires a plan and focus.

Have a plan. Have a plan for handling these shots. When you see the wide-open court, aim for a target. Hit a short angle shot aiming for the area where the service line meets the alley to move your opponent off the court; or hit the ball deep down the line, come into net, and volley. A plan helps you stay focused when you hit and ultimately makes you a more accurate player.

Use finesse. Hitting power shots is not the only way to win points; you can also use finesse. People seem to forget that they do not have to smack the ball when they have an easy shot. Remember, you do not have to crush the weak serve. In fact, one winning strategy is to hit your opponent a short ball after you are hit a soft shot. To set yourself up when you get a drop shot, hit a drop shot over the net right in front of you. If your opponent reaches your drop shot it will probably be hit it up and you can volley it away. Your opponent may be so surprised that you controlled the ball instead of smashing it that your drop shot may win the point. Now it is your opponent's turn to be frustrated about missing an easy shot. Turnabout is fair play.

Stay in the match. Sometimes dreaded easy shots are the turning point in a match. This can happen if you get so upset that you missed that you lose your concentration. That's a real shame because it means you are beating yourself. If you miss an easy shot, it's OK to be mad, but then remind yourself what you need to do next time and prepare for the next point. Acknowledge the shot; then move on with the rest of the match. The best players stay focused and positive even if they make an error.

Summary

An easy shot is a nice treat when you are playing a match. But missing one can really throw you off your game. To hit the dreaded easy shot well, you must be on your toes. Literally. Make sure you are in position for each ball. Don't get upset if you miss the ball once in a while. Practice. If you have a plan, use finesse some of the time, and stay in the match, you will find that you are taking full advantage of your easy-shot opportunities.

5

THE BIG POINTS

It could have happened in a recent game. You're playing well, relaxed, and having fun. Everything's fine until you realize that you need these next few points. Right now. These points. Suddenly it happens. .... It's not the way it was before—you're not quite in position for the ball, you're thinking too much, and your serves are going out. You find yourself distracted by the players on the next court, by people behind the court. Maybe you even start worrying about the bounces you are getting.

Does this scenario sound familiar? Most people have felt it at one time or another. These changes are caused by the extra pressure and problems that arrive with big points. Playing big points well is one of the things that makes you a better, even a great, tennis player. See the on-court drills in *Focus Under Pressure* on page 38 to help you focus, use your strengths, and play big points like a champion.

Focus

When you're playing great, focusing is easy. Some people feel as if "it just happens"; they don't have to think or work at playing well, they're just "on." The problems arise when your focus is off. Luckily, when your focus slips, there are strategies you can use to help bring yourself back into that automatic state (see *Key Words* on the next page).

About Focus

It would be so easy if you could snap your fingers and say "FOCUS, FOCUS, FOCUS," and "poof" you would be back playing your best tennis. Unfortunately, the more you think about focusing, the less you are paying attention to the ball. The problem is that thinking about focusing is not the same as being focused. So what do you do?

Once you recognize that you have lost focus, you are on your way back up. Self-awareness, recognizing that something is wrong with your mental game, allows you to do something about it. You should realize, however, that focusing is not a simple activity. It involves both your mind and your body. If either part is not working, then your focus can be disrupted.

Physical Focus

Many people find starting with the body is the easiest way to regain focus. Here's a great way to physically focus: Stop, take some slow, deep breaths, and clear your mind (see chapter 3 for more details on deep breathing). The beauty of deep, slow breathing is that you can use it at almost any time during your match—on changeovers, before your serve, and even before you receive. When you do use deep, slow breathing before you receive—beware—make sure that you turn your back or step

KEY WORDS

Key words (and phrases) can help you to focus your energy and reach beyond your usual physical and mental limits. You will probably want to select calming key words for high-pressure situations and energizing key words to help stay motivated when you are tired or distracted. Select key words (see examples below) that you feel comfortable with and use them during practices and matches.

Calming key words	Energizing key words
Smooth	Power
Loose	Explode
Easy	Rrrowr!
Fluid	Yeah!
Breathe	Attack
Relax	Pounce
Calm	Get going!
	I'm here to play
	I can stay out here longer
	I want it!
	Be tough
	I can play as long as it takes

aside so that the server knows that you are not ready yet.

Once your breathing has helped you to calm down, you need to regroup and reorient yourself to the match. Shift your weight onto your toes or jump in place. Moving your feet may seem like a simple way to regain focus, but it works. Watch the pros playing tennis, and you'll see that their weight is on the balls of their feet when they are returning serve (some even jog in place).

If you lose focus because of your own mistakes, you may find yourself becoming frustrated and "out of sync." Take a few practice swings to recover your rhythm and to loosen up your strokes. These physical steps—breathing, moving your feet, and taking practice swings—help you regain focus, especially if they are used with the following mental tips.

Mental Focus

Many times when you lose focus, your mind is going a mile a minute. Those are the times you are thinking about everything in the world *except* the next point. To regain your focus on tennis, you first have to bring yourself "back to the court" and what you are doing. Simplify your thoughts by picking one aspect of the game to concentrate on. Keep it basic. You might think "hit the ball to their backhand" or "hit crosscourt." As easy as this sounds, you'll find that when you have a specific plan, nontennis thoughts will fade away by themselves.

On some days you may find that physical focus is all that you need; on other days you will need to pull out all the stops. When you need an extra boost, remember that you have time to work on regaining focus on changeovers.

FOCUS UNDER PRESSURE

Skill objective: Improve play in big points
Psychological objective: Stay competitive, relaxed, and focused

Procedure

1. Play a set with a practice partner.
2. Use regular scoring until one player reaches "40." If the player with "40" wins the next point, he wins the game. If the player with "40" loses that point, however, his score in the game goes back to 0, while the opponent's score remains the same.
3. Continue playing the game (and set) until one player wins.

Options

1. Use one serve only (no second serve).
2. Start the set score at 3–3.

Tips

1. The scoring can be confusing at first so say the score aloud for each point.
2. Notice how you do when you play the big points (when one player has "40") aggressively and when you play for consistency.

Changeovers

On changeovers, use the extra time to improve your focus. After a few deep breaths and a drink of water, evaluate your performance and your strategy. Is your opponent hitting great forehands? Then go to the backhand. Are you getting hurt when you hit short balls? Then keep the ball high and deep. Don't beat yourself up about past errors; it's a waste of time and not helpful. Use the changeover as a new start and come out of it relaxed, rehydrated, and refocused.

The more you use these techniques, the easier you will find it to focus. Working on your focus in practice as well as in matches will help you to focus better and faster.

BIG POINTS MADE EASY IN FOUR STEPS

If you can relax and recover between points, you will be properly ener-gized and focused. At first, these steps may feel forced. With practice, you will find that they will help you to recover and that your consistency and confidence will improve.

After the point:
1. Release emotions.
   — Give yourself a "yeah" for a great point.
   — Release frustration (within the rules) if you need to.
2. Relax.
   — Let the past point go.
   — Take some deep, slow breaths (see *Deep, Slow Breathing* in chapter 3).
3. Evaluate the last point.
   — Consider what worked and why.
   — Select your strategy for the next point.
4. Refocus.
   — Remind yourself of your strategy.
   — Get into position to play.
   — Move your feet.
   — Watch the ball.
5. Play!

Use Your Strengths

Mastering the art of focusing is not all you need to do on the big points. That's because big points take on a life of their own. The court looks smaller, your legs feel heavier, and your arm is tighter. We do things differently because it's THE BIG POINT. But the big point is just a regular point with an ego. You can deflate it if you stick with what brought you this far (see *Big Points Made Easy in Four Steps* on the previous page).

Having a mental reminder can be helpful on big points. You may want to think "stick with what brung ya" or "use what works" before the point starts. The idea is to remind yourself to go with your strengths. If you are a steady, patient player, stay patient and wait for your opponent to make an error. If you are an aggressive player, stay aggressive. Continue to use the weapon that has been winning points for you.

It is a simple and smart strategy to use what you do best in your matches. Amazingly, many tennis players fail to use their strengths to their advantage on big points. Steady baseliners get to big points and suddenly try to hit the John McEnroe baseline overhead for a winner. Serve-and-volleyers hesitate and start staying back to rally with their opponents. Don't become a victim of this kind of big-point madness.

Of course steady players shouldn't just hit the ball down the middle, and aggressive players should not try for the total glory shot to make the highlight film. Each player should continue to do what won points throughout the match. One last tip for everyone—save your new twist serve or touch volley for some other time.

Summary

Playing big points well gives your tennis game an extra edge. Work on the physical and mental aspects of focusing, and you are off to a good start. During the point, be confident and stick with what has been winning for you. If you are able to incorporate these tips into your game, you'll find yourself looking forward to the big points because you will be the one winning them!

6

THE BIG MATCHES

Sometimes when you play it's more for fun and practice. Then there are the matches that matter. You want to play well, you want to play great, but what can you do to make sure that you "have it" when the competition begins?

The good news is that there are a number of strategies that you can use to help you play your best when you need to. The bad news is that they will take some extra preparation on your part. Overall, though, considering the time and energy that you invest in playing, you will probably find that these extras—scouting your opponent, visualizing, practicing like you play, and warming up—are worth the additional effort.

Scouting Your Opponent

If possible, scout your opponents prior to your matches. Go watch them compete. After each match you play, you can also record your impressions of your opponents' games and keep that information for future use.

I (JVR) remember playing Julie N. in a tournament. I was nervous because we had played a close match previously. When I went back over what I had written about that match, I remembered that she was a big topspin hitter who moved really well side to side, but had trouble moving forward and backward in the court. With that information (and extra confidence) in hand, I did something that I don't usually do: I hit her a lot of short balls (especially after hitting deep shots). I won the match easily.

The scouting reports in *Scouting Report on Pat* and *Scouting Report on Chris* will give you some ideas of what to look for when you are scouting your opponents. You can also ask people who have played your opponent what to expect, what your opponent's strengths and weaknesses are. If you play this opponent regularly, think about your past matches in more detail. All tennis players have their "go to" shot and the shot they try to avoid or hide. Your job is to find out what your opponent has and to figure out how you are going to play against it. Scouting your opponent prepares you for the match. It gives you a chance to think about how you want to play *before* you are under pressure.

Visualization

Once you have some information about your opponent, you can develop a strategy or plan to use in your match. If your opponent is a big power hitter, you may decide to hit some soft shots to vary the rhythm of the points. If your opponent is

SCOUTING REPORT ON PAT

1. *Name of opponent:* Pat
2. *Date of match:* March 19
3. *Score of match:* W 6–4, 6–1
4. *Court surface:* hard
5. *Weather conditions:* indoors
6. *Right- or left-handed:* right-handed
7. *Forehand:* uses big topspin, typically goes crosscourt, but can go down the line
8. *Backhand:* two-handed, typically goes down the line, slow in getting feet set up
9. *Volleys:* weak on the backhand side, trouble with low volleys
10. *Overheads:* generally good, but doesn't always angle the ball away
11. *Serves (first and second):*
    First—big and flat, gets it in 50% of the time
    Second—some spin, but weak
12. *Movement:* moves well side to side, slow coming forward, good moving back, very quick, gets to a lot of balls
13. *Style of play:* consistent player who likes to hit hard
14. *Best shot:* forehand, likes to go crosscourt with topspin
15. *Weakest shot:* trouble with low backhands
16. *Suggested strategy:* Work the backhand with low slicing balls; mix it up between short balls and lobs; block back the first serve and step in for the second; expect the ball to come back.
17. *Other comments:* honest on calls, a fun match to play

steady, you may want to come to the net so that you can put the ball away and end the points. You may also want to develop a plan for yourself to protect your weaknesses. You can try out the plan using visualization. Visualization is creating or recreating an experience in your mind (see *Visualization*).

SCOUTING REPORT ON CHRIS

1. *Name of opponent:* Chris
2. *Date of match:* May 27
3. *Score of match:* L 6–3, 7–5
4. *Court surface:* hard
5. *Weather conditions:* outdoors, hot and humid
6. *Right- or left-handed:* right-handed
7. *Forehand:* flat but slices the short balls
8. *Backhand:* one-handed slice, hits short angles crosscourt and deeper shots down the line
9. *Volleys:* very strong on both sides, has some trouble when ball is hit right at the body
10. *Overheads:* solid, goes crosscourt, a little trouble with really high lobs
11. *Serves (first and second):*
    First—topspin with occasional wide slice to forehand
    Second—topspin, usually right at my body
12. *Movement:* moves very well to the net, a little slower on the fore-hand side
13. *Style of play:* serve-and-volleyer who likes to attack the net, fore-hand can be shaky sometimes.
14. *Best shot:* volleys and short backhand (angles it away crosscourt)
15. *Weakest shot:* high, deep forehands
16. *Suggested strategy:* Keep the ball deep and keep Chris off the net. Hit high and deep to the forehand as often as possible. Anticipate short-angled shot off backhands. Mix up passing shots with high, deep lobs.
17. *Other comments:* Work on improving my own fitness. I ran out of steam at the end of the second set. Chris had a funny toss on first serves that threw me off a little. Stick to my game plan.

Visualization off the court. Many people find it easiest to vi-sualize themselves playing tennis when they are relaxed and in a quiet place. You can try visualizing before you go to sleep. If visualizing before bed prevents you from sleeping well, you

VISUALIZATION

Visualization is easiest when relaxed. Try closing your eyes and taking several deep, slow breaths. You may want to have a partner read the following in a slow, relaxing voice. You can also tape-record it yourself. Feel free to modify the script to match your game situation.

Imagine yourself arriving at the tennis courts . . . hear the sounds of tennis balls and racquets . . . see people playing . . . feel the air, the environment . . . notice all the things around you . . . as you look around, begin to pay attention to your own emotions . . . enjoy anticipating the match . . . notice the feelings in your body . . . a little bit nervous, but ready to play . . . remember that this is how you usually feel before a match . . .

See yourself going out to your court . . . ready to warm up . . . racquet in hand . . . feel yourself hit smooth, powerful shots . . . you are moving well . . . the ball goes where you want . . . you feel relaxed and confident . . . you sense the rhythm of the game . . . bounce, hit, bounce, hit . . . you say positive things to yourself . . . "I am hitting great" . . . "I am focused" . . . "I am consistent" . . . "I am staying positive" . . . "If I get frustrated, I can just let it go" . . . "I am confident and secure" . . . sense your energy as the match is about to begin . . . feel strong, determined, ready . . .

Now the match begins . . . you are quick about the court . . . your feet are light . . . your shots accurate and powerful . . . your concentration comes easily . . . you hit the ball just where you want . . . the rhythm of the game flows . . . you feel the perfection of your shots . . .

You are serving . . . you toss the ball and reach up to hit . . . your swing smooth and strong . . . the return comes back and you get into position . . . your feet are light . . . movement is easy . . . you hit a deep shot crosscourt and win the point . . . you feel good about your game . . . you serve again and are ready for the return . . . you put away the short ball . . . aggressive, smooth, closing out points and games . . . confident and relaxed . . . you can overcome anything . . . the match continues . . . you focus on the ball and on each point alone . . . completely in the moment . . . a part of each shot . . . even if you lose the point . . . you are ready and playing and fine . . .

Savor these feelings for a while . . . the rhythm, the confidence, the fun . . . when you are ready, slowly see the court start to fade . . . the players grow dim . . . the sounds more distant . . . notice how your energy and composure remain . . . even as you start to return to the here-and-now, you sense extra confidence and focus . . . you will be completely ready for your next match . . . you will play your best . . . you are ready.

might try it in the shower, at lunch, or during another quiet time of day.

Some people worry that they'll play badly if they visualize themselves making an error. It's OK to visualize an error, but you may want to try to correct the error in your mind. Replay the point in slow motion if necessary. If you find that you lose when you mentally try a particular strategy against your opponent, then try another strategy. The beauty of visualization is that you can switch gears, use "do overs," try out new strategies, and never lose a real point!

Visualization on the court. When you are playing a match, you can also use visualization. One way to incorporate visualization into your game is to use it before you serve and return.

When you are serving, use a regular routine. You can start your routine when you get into position to serve. You may say the score aloud, take a deep breath, bounce the ball a few times, and then visualize your serve. Visualizing helps keep you focused and reminds you of your strategy, such as serve the ball out wide or right at your opponent's body or use extra topspin.

You may also visualize before a return. Some players visualize by actually taking a practice swing; others tell themselves where they want to hit the ball (i.e., they think "crosscourt"); still others use more complex mental imagery. When you visualize a return, you can see yourself hitting an ideal return. You can also visualize yourself hitting the return that has been giving you trouble or the return you are expecting to hit on the next shot. After you visualize, and before your opponent serves to you, refocus on the match. Visualization helps you to gain confidence and focus, but after you visualize, regroup and concentrate to return the ball.

Practice Like You Play

Lots of people say that they play great in practice, can even visualize themselves playing well, but can't seem to play the way they want to in big matches. The problem is often this: In practice, people don't practice what they need for matches. That's why we suggest that you practice in the way you want to play.

If you are going to be playing a 2-hour match then you need to practice playing competitive tennis for 2 hours. Try to make the practice seem like a "real" match: Keep your warm-up brief, spin to see who will serve first, change ends on odd games. If your big match will be indoors, then practice indoors. If you will be playing in front of a crowd, then ask some people to be your "crowd" in practice. If you will be playing a lefty, then find a lefty (or a slicer, or a lobber, etc.) to practice against. The more familiar you are with the length of play, the environment, and the type of player, the better you will do in your match. Sometimes you can't arrange all the practice that you would like. When this happens, use the best substitute you can find. Watch tennis on television, take practice swings with your racquet in hand, stretch well. Anything is better than nothing. The more you practice like you want to play, the fewer surprises there will be on match day.

Warm-up

If you do not scout your opponents, your first look at their game will be during the warm-up. What you must do during the warm-up is learn about your opponent's strengths and weaknesses. This means that you should be focusing on the other player. Of course you can't focus on your opponent if you are trying to warm yourself up. Here's a tip: Warm up before the warm-up. Hit with a friend or use a backboard. If you can't get to the courts to hit, at least jog a little bit, stretch, and take practice swings so that you are as ready as possible to play. The more ready you are, the more able you are to learn about your opponent. The more you focus on your opponent, the more information you will gather, the more you can anticipate your opponent's style of play or hitting patterns, and the more effective your game plan will be.

Scouting your opponent, visualizing, practicing correctly, and using the warm-up to your advantage will help you to get off on the right foot on match day. Once the match starts, there are several techniques that can keep the ball rolling: Use what you learned when you scouted your opponent, be flexible, and play the percentages.

Playing the Big Match

When it comes to playing the big match, your preparation gives you confidence. Use this extra confidence and knowledge. If you observe during your scouting or warm-up that your opponent does not move well for the short ball, you can anticipate that he will have trouble with a combination of drop shots and lobs. So, drop shot and lob him to death. On some days, however, you may find that the drop shot and lob combination is not working for you. If you prepare for this possibility, you will be able to switch gears and go from Plan A to Plan B. If you're not hitting a shot well, don't overuse it! You need to use your strengths while going to your opponent's weaknesses. Find a combination of shots that fits both categories, and you will find yourself on the winning side.

Playing the opponent you've played before. Sometimes playing an opponent you are familiar with can work to your *dis*advantage. You may feel intimidated, especially if you lost to that person last time. On the other hand, you may be overconfident, especially if you won your previous matches. Remember that this match is a new opportunity and start off fresh.

Think about your opponent and decide how you are going to play this time. Past experience allows you to fine tune your game plan and to make it very specific. If it is someone you have lost to, you may want to change your strategy. When playing very steady opponents, people often overhit. If you do this consistently, you'll look like a big gun, but you'll probably be losing. Think of a new game plan. You might want to try for more consistency, perhaps hitting lobs or deep shots. You might want to try to come to the net more.

If you are playing someone whom you have beaten, remember that each match is a new opportunity. It is a good bet to use the strategy that worked before. If you discover that it is not working this time, be flexible, regroup, and try something new. Remember, the match outcome is never set in stone. Adjust your strategy to play with the strengths and weaknesses that are present on this match day.

What to do when you don't know what to do. We've been talking about all these great strategies that you have developed. Sometimes you don't have a game plan or know what to do to win a match. Being consistent, moving your opponent, hitting to your opponent's weakness, and mixing up the pace of the ball are some of the best strategies you can use.

The person who hits the ball over the net and in the court more times than the opponent does wins the match. To play consistently, you need to focus on being in position for every shot. If you hit the ball over the net five times during a point, you will win most points. If it helps, you can count the shots as you are hitting. Counting can settle your game into a rhythm. To play consistently, you should also play the percentages. Hitting crosscourt is a high-percentage shot because you are hitting the ball over the lowest part of the net and into the widest part of the court.

Another thing you can do is make your opponent run. For most people, hitting the ball on the run is harder. That means they are more likely to miss the shot and become fatigued sooner. Playing tired opponents makes your job easier. Get them running by hitting the ball from side to side. Remember, you can also make them run by hitting the ball short and then deep. This simple strategy can be very effective. Steffi Graf uses this strategy in all her matches.

Simple strategies are the easiest to use during competition. Sometimes you just need a basic plan, such as hitting to your opponent's backhand (or weaker side) whenever you can. You can also try hitting the ball back the way that your opponent hit it to you (crosscourt back crosscourt, down the line back down the line).

Against power players one of the most effective strategies is to change the pace of the ball. Hit a hard shot, and then follow it with a soft shot. If you can hit slice or topspin, try adding that to the mix. Changing the pace breaks up your opponent's rhythm.

Changing Your Strategy

When you are under big match pressure, you want to see positive results immediately. In your efforts to play well, make sure that you remember to give your strategy time to work. If your strategy is to hit to your opponent's backhand and you are blasted with a backhand winner, don't give up on your plan yet. It may be that you need to improve your focus (see chapter 5) rather than change your game. On the other hand, don't stick with a losing game plan indefinitely. When should you change strategies? A rule of thumb is to consider switching if you are down 4–0 or 4–1. That way, if your new strategy (Plan B) doesn't work, you will have time to try your Plan C in the next set. There is no magical time to change a strategy, but most people tend to change too soon.

Give your strategy time to work and pay attention to what is happening in the match. Figure out why your strategy is not working, and you will have a clue about what new strategy you should try. Maybe your opponent's weak backhand is grooved because you've been going there all time. Maybe your opponent is anticipating where you are going to hit, especially if you are hitting everything crosscourt. Maybe what you thought was the weaker shot really wasn't so bad after all. Use a new strategy based on your assessment of what has been working for you in the match.

Chris was playing in a big match and had put himself into a perfect position to win. He had taken a hard-fought first set and was ahead 5–4 in the second. All of a sudden, the jitters hit. He got his feet moving to get rid of the nervousness, but it wasn't enough. He tried to calm down, but in his excitement, he forgot his tennis mental game. His tennis mental strategy was to imagine that he was behind instead of ahead. Then he would feel like an underdog who could pull the match out. The underdog, calm and focused. Instead of playing like an underdog, Chris kept thinking about how close the match was, and he ended up losing the set 7–5. Lesson learned, he now knows how important it is to stick with his mental game.

Summary

When the big matches come around, you want to be ready to play. You will find that if you scout your opponent, visualize, practice for the match, and warm up, then you will be at your best. Once the match starts, use what you learned when you scouted your opponent, be flexible, and play the percentages. If you take the extra time to treat every competitive match like a big match, then you will find yourself winning more often.

WHAT TO DO ABOUT THOSE NASTY THINGS YOU CAN'T CONTROL

SECTION III

7

HOW TO HANDLE ENVIRONMENTAL CONDITIONS

You like to play tennis as much as the next person. In fact, you are so motivated that you are playing in a tournament. When you arrive at the courts, you are ready, but where did the seemingly subzero temperatures, rotten lighting, or gale force winds come from? These are the worst possible conditions. You can't hit anything. HELP!

A major problem with tennis is that it is never played in a perfect environment. There are always distractions. That's the bad news. The good news is that your opponent has to contend with the same conditions that you face. There are several tactics for dealing with the challenges posed by poor playing conditions. If you expect some distractions, prepare for the conditions (see *Tennis Bag Essentials* on page 59), and remember that your opponent is suffering too, then you will be better able to deal with weather, lighting, and court surface surprises.

Weather

The weather affects you when you are playing outdoors. It also affects you if you are playing indoors and have to travel to your game. Check the weather forecast or spend a few minutes in front of the Weather Channel, and you will be prepared for whatever Mother Nature throws your way.

Travel to matches. Weather is a problem only in extreme climates, right? Wrong! Perfect weather could mean big delays in travel in some places. You may have to contend with beach traffic or road construction projects. In cold weather, you may encounter rainy, snowy, or icy conditions that make travel hazardous and slow. Plan your trip so that you arrive about an hour before the match to give yourself plenty of time to warm up and prepare to play. This preparation will leave you a cushion of time in case you are lost or caught in traffic. We know you may be thinking, "I don't want to be too early because I get nervous waiting to play." If you are nervous waiting or watching other people play tennis before your match, then you need something else to do. You can read a book, take a shower, run, stretch, or listen to music—anything that keeps you relaxed and ready. Remember, it is always better to be at the courts early than to be defaulted because you are late.

When you arrive at the courts for your match, be prepared. Make sure that you bring supplies for tennis conditions that are cooler, warmer, and windier than you expect in case the weather report is off target, or the indoor club has problems with its heating and cooling system.

Hot days. For hot days outdoors, it is important to be prepared with plenty of water, sunscreen, sunglasses, and a hat. It wouldn't hurt to bring extra shirts and socks along in case you need a change during the match. A towel to wipe your sweaty brow and an extra grip for your racquet in case yours gets slippery would also be nice. You may find that you do not like to play wearing a hat or sunglasses. Practice with them before you give up totally. Remember, you want to live a long and healthy life, and minimizing your sun exposure is a good idea. If you become used to the equipment in practice, you will be all set for your matches.

On hot days, it is important to stay hydrated. Players suffering from heat stroke have to default. Medical alert! Don't wait until you feel thirsty to start drinking. You need water even before you start to gasp for it. The best thing to do is drink plenty of water on every changeover.

On extremely hot days, you may be tempted to skip your warm-up. It can be so hot that you don't feel like moving. You may figure that your muscles are already warm and loosened up. Remember, it is going to be hard to get yourself moving in the match on this kind of day. You need to jump-start the system. You will find any warm-up you do will put you at an advantage.

Cold days. You may find yourself playing tennis on surprisingly cold days. The key to cold-match attire is to dress in layers. As you warm up, you can strip down and still be comfortable.

On very cold days, you will find that the tennis balls do not bounce to their regular height. Rubber loses its elasticity in the cold, which means that you are going to have to bend more to reach low balls. On cold days, warming up before you play will enable you to bend more easily and reduce your risk of injury. Warming up will also keep you from standing around and shivering. If you look as if you are ready to play on a cold day, you might even intimidate your opponent, who is probably standing around shivering.

Windy days. The wind can be a real challenge. It can blow your great shots out and give your opponent's mediocre shots the extra oomph they need to get by you. The wind can drive you crazy.

Windy days are not bad (and are even good) if you are prepared for them. Here is what you should do. On a windy day, warm up on both sides of the net. Usually you just hit on one side, but on a windy day you will need to know how to adjust. Take some practice serves on both ends of the court too. This will be a big help, especially if you are a high tosser. You may need to modify your toss (toss it lower). Remember, if you have a bad toss on your serve, you can catch the ball and toss it again. You can also wait a few moments until the wind dies down a bit before you serve.

I (JVR) actually like playing on windy days. I know that if I am patient, the wind can frustrate my opponent and make my job easier. I remember playing an outdoor tournament on courts right in the middle of a big field. The wind picked up speed as it blew—big gusts that almost knocked me off my feet. My opponent, who was a better player than I, said, "Are we actually going to play today?" I agreed the wind was terrible, but secretly smiled. The wind was making her crazy, and I knew that her mind was not on tennis. Sure enough, I won the first set. I did everything that I could that set to prevent her from settling into a rhythm. I lobbed, I hit drop shots, I whacked the ball. When I missed, I kept my cool; I could see that the wind was actually working to my advantage. Unfortunately, in the second set she settled down. Once she started hitting for real, I was in trouble. I was destined for a three-set loss when the wind kicked up to an even higher level. "Come on, hurricane," I thought, and with a few wild bounces going my way, I managed to take the second set 6–4.

The best way to improve your play on windy days is to practice on windy days. You will probably find that it is to your benefit to stand a bit inside the baseline and come to the net when your opponent is hitting into the wind. That's because your opponent's shots will have less power. You can be ready at net to volley and take advantage of weak shots. When you are hitting into the wind, hit flat and hard. Drop shots are extra effective when hit into the wind, too. If the wind is behind you, try some lobs (they will blow deep) but use extra topspin to keep the ball in.

Sometimes the wind blows across the court, which poses another set of challenges. Plan to hit some balls deep so that the wind takes them into your opponent's body. Hit short angle shots with the wind to make them especially tough to return. No matter what the wind does, take quick, small steps, and you can adjust your position as the ball blows around. To use the wind to your advantage, you need to practice, adjust to the conditions on your side of the court, and be alert to changes in the wind patterns. On windy days especially, the mentally alert player is the one who has the edge.

TENNIS BAG ESSENTIALS

1. Tennis racquets (at least two in case you break a string)
2. Water bottle or sport drink
3. Towel, sweatbands
4. Extra socks, shirt(s), shorts, sweatshirt
5. Energy snacks
6. First aid basics: Band-Aids, tape, aspirin, tissues
7. Sunscreen, sunglasses, hat, lip balm
8. Additional equipment: tennis balls (to warm up with), extra shoes, extra tennis grip, extra vibration dampener, string

Lighting

Being able to see the ball makes it much easier to hit. Unfortunately, sometimes you have to play when you can't really see. It would be great if we could give you Superman's vision, but we can't. The best we can do is help you prepare for low light and glare conditions when you play.

Low light. Many tennis clubs have lousy lighting systems. Some are poorly designed, and some are poorly maintained. Whatever the cause, it can be hard to see when you are playing under the lights. It can also be hard to see if your match starts very early in the morning or goes on into dusk. The ball often seems to come out of nowhere, and you end up feeling as though you can't hit a thing.

In low light, first do all that you can to improve your vision. Make sure you have enough saline solution for your contact lenses. Take off your hat and sunglasses if you are wearing them. If you are playing outdoors, ask if the court lights can be turned on. Getting these basics under control could be all that you need.

Once you have things as bright as you can, you may still find it hard to play. When the lighting is dim, you spot the ball later than usual and have less time to prepare. To compensate, get to the ball quickly. Shorten your backswing so that you are ready to hit early. Even though you are adjusting to the conditions, make sure you still use your full follow-through to put spin on the ball and keep it in. There is no perfect way to play in the dark, but if you practice in these conditions, you will find that you will play better when you have to.

Bright light. On sunny days, you may have the problem of too much light. The glare can make it hard to see the ball. Bring sunglasses and a hat or visor to wear. Blocking the sun lets you focus on the ball and play better tennis.

On sunny days, serving can be really tough. The sun often seems to be in the exact place that you have to look when you serve. Even if your serve goes in, it can be hard to return the next shot because all you see is spots. On these types of days, you will have to modify your serve. You may want to slightly adjust your toss so that you don't lose the ball in the sun. You may try moving along the baseline to find a spot where the sun is not quite so bad. If you are extremely coordinated, you can use your tossing arm as a sun shield. If you need to, you can serve the ball underhanded. Remember, it is always helpful to see the ball when you serve!

Once you put your serve in play, remember to use the sun to your advantage. If your opponents come to the net on the sunny side, lob. They can't see the ball well and, even if they hit the overhead, may have difficulty seeing the next shot. When they are serving on the sunny side, realize that they will be briefly blinded after they serve. Hit unexpected shots with extra spin or angles across the court. Playing when it is really bright out can be challenging. If you consider it a challenge, you will rise to the occasion and play well.

COURT SURFACES

Hard courts
- Attack the ball when possible.
- Hit the ball into the open court.
- Practice on the courts where you will be competing. Not all hard courts are the same.

Clay
- Practice sliding.
- Hit shots behind your opponent to wrong-foot him or her.
- Expect long points on this slow surface.
- Use topspin, slice, and drop shots to mix things up.

Grass
- Expect strange bounces.
- Expect balls to come low and fast.
- Attack returns and get to the net.

Court Surface

If you are competing in the United States, most of the matches that you play will be on some type of hard court. There are some clubs left with carpet surfaces or the occasional outdoor clay court or Har-Tru (green clay) setup. For the most part, however, hard courts are what you will see.

Knowing the surface you are playing on can help you prepare for your match (see *Court Surfaces* above). Clay courts require that you slide to the ball. Be sure to practice sliding. On clay, try hitting shots behind your opponents, they will struggle to change direction quickly. The bounce on clay tends to be slow. That means many balls will come back and the points will probably be longer than usual. Use topspin, slice, and drop shots to mix things up. Come mentally prepared for a long match, and you will be ready to take full advantage of clay courts. Grass courts have a low, fast bounce. You can get weird bounces on grass. Attack returns and go to the net. That way you will not be at the mercy of the turf. Hard courts provide consistent bounces, so when you play on hard courts, you can stand up on the baseline and attack the ball. Using your serve as a weapon and hitting the ball into the open court with powerful shots are also effective. Beware, hard court surfaces are similar, but are not all the same. On some courts, the ball seems to skid and stay low. On other courts, the ball bounces way up. If you have the chance to practice on the courts where you will be competing, you will be at an advantage. Practicing on the court will help you adjust to the tempo and become used to the conditions.

You will find it easiest to play on all surfaces if you have solid footing. Make sure that your shoes are in good condition and that you still have some tread left. If you are playing on grass or clay, wear shoes that are appropriate for the surface and you will be ready to go.

Summary

Getting ready to play your best tennis requires you to work on your strokes, strategy, and mental game. This includes expecting whatever Mother Nature and the tennis club might throw your way. If you plan for weather, lighting, and court surface challenges, you can concentrate on tennis instead of your frustration and aggravation with the lousy conditions. Players who are prepared and focus their energy on playing are the ones who win.

OVERCOMING HUMAN CHALLENGES

(LINE CALLS, GAMESMANSHIP, SPECTATORS)

THAT WAS **IN**!

You're deep into the match. You hit a clear winner, and then you can't believe your ears. "Out! You called that out?" you ask your opponent in disbelief. The ball was obviously in. You keep playing, but are distracted and double fault the next point. People start cheering. Your opponent's friends are clapping every time you miss a ball. You like to play tennis, but this is out of control.

Playing tennis involves all kinds of challenges. To handle tennis problems with your concentration, footwork, strokes, and strategy see the chapters in section II "Oh the Pressure!" and section V "What to Do If It All Falls Apart." Keep reading this chapter if you want to deal better with questionable line calls, gamesmanship, and spectators.

Dealing With Bad Line Calls

In most matches, both you and your opponent call the lines honestly. You relinquish the point if you do not see the ball clearly out. Occasionally, however, you play someone who seems to use the motto, "When in doubt, call it out." You are amazed when you hear the call. "No, not again! That was the third time that one of my great shots was called out!" How you handle the situation from here can determine the outcome of your match. Some people just let the calls go; some people question their opponents' line calls; some people mentally take credit for the points that they think they should have won; and some people ask for a line judge. Deciding in advance how to handle this type of situation will help you relax and play your game (see *Line Call Pressure Drill*, next page, for a drill to help you deal with bad line calls).

Let it go. When line calls are the issue in a match, remember that the rules of tennis are clear. If the ball bounces on your opponent's side of the net, then your opponent makes the line call. Probably the best thing to do about a questionable line call is "let it go." If you need extra help letting it go, try the procedure in *Big Points Made Easy in Four Steps* in chapter 5. Remember, one point does not decide the outcome of the match.

Question your opponent. When a bad line call is so upsetting that you just have to do something, ask if your opponent is "sure" about the call. Presumably, your opponent could then revoke the incorrect call and give you the point. We can't remember playing opponents who changed their calls after being asked "Are you sure?" but we imagine it could happen. Usually, asking "Are you sure?" puts your opponent on notice that you are concerned about the line calls and that you thought the ball was in. Perhaps your opponent will be more careful and more generous about calls during subsequent points. Asking about the call allows you to vent some of your frustration. Blowing off steam is good if you can then regroup and prepare for the next point. Acknowledge your frustration and move on. Remember, if you stay angry you will be in no position to play the rest of the match.

If you don't move on, you will get into trouble. For example, you may think to yourself, "I should have won that point." Although your opponent is ahead in the game 40-30, you may be thinking that the "true" score should give you the lead. Things get complicated when you are keeping two sets of scores. You stop focusing on the ball and aren't ready to play. Keeping track of the "real" score while counting the number of bad calls you get is guaranteed to hurt your game.

Sometimes you run into a different sort of opponent. I (CSB) played a guy named Rick B. whose line calls made me crazy. He would call "out" balls "in" especially on serve. I would serve, assume the ball was out, and prepare to hit my second serve. He would hit the ball back and then walk to the other side to receive serve for the next point. I'd ask him if the ball was out, but he would say, "No, it was in. Great serve." He won several points like that before I readied myself to hit the next ball even when I thought my serve was out.

LINE CALL PRESSURE DRILL

Psychological objective: Maintain concentration when you get bad line calls

Procedure
1. Play a set with a practice partner.
2. During the match your practice partner makes a "bad" line call (e.g., calls an "in" ball "out").
3. Your practice partner wins that free point.
4. Allow your practice partner three free points per set.

Options
1. Give your practice partner more free points.
2. If your practice partner wins the point after taking a free point, your practice partner wins the game.

Ask for a line judge. If poor line calls turn out to be an ongoing problem in an unofficiated match, the best solution is to ask for a line judge. A line judge could be a tournament director, unaffiliated spectator, or other neutral person who is asked to stand at the net post during the match. Line judges don't make the line calls, but if a player questions a call, they rule on it. Having a line judge can help you to focus on your tennis and take your mind off the frustration that you feel with your opponent (see *Strategy Drill*, next page, for a drill to help you focus on your tennis). Line judges usually act as a calming influence on both players.

You may feel uncomfortable requesting a line judge, and sometimes line judges are not available. In these cases, the best option is to forget about your opponent's line calls and aim more for the middle of the court. That way line calls will not be a factor in the match. If you absolutely can't let it go, then stop playing. Being overly aggravated while you play tennis is just not worth it. Some people suggest making bad line calls back to an opponent who makes bad line calls for you. Wrong. Cheating is against the rules of tennis in all cases. Play hard, play fair, have fun, and you will find that your opponents will generally do the same.

Dealing With Gamesmanship

You've probably heard the old joke. There are two kinds of people in the world: those who categorize people into two groups and those who don't. With tennis, it seems as if there are two kinds of opponents, those who use gamesmanship (e.g., purposely distract you, mix up the score) and those who don't. If you play someone who uses mental tricks, you may find yourself and your tennis game sorely tested. Don't let these opponents get the better of you. Scout your opponent, develop a plan, and you will be on your way to managing gamesmanship problems.

Maybe you are reading this and thinking, "Gamesmanship, hmmmm, that sounds interesting. After all, any advantage I could get for myself would be nice." Although you might be tempted to try these tactics, gamesmanship should not be your mode of play. Gamesmanship is unsporting. Also, many players who use gamesmanship actually end up distracting themselves as much as their opponents. They end up losing the advantage they hoped to gain. They also earn reputations as players who are always "pulling something," and no one wants to play with them.

You may be thinking that using gamesmanship is a cheap shot. Why do players do that? The answer is simple: They do it because gamesmanship sometimes does help them win. For example, if you are playing a match and feel that your opponent is purposely stalling—maybe using the old "tie the shoe" trick to make you wait to serve when you are on a roll—you will probably become frustrated and even a little bit mad. As this frustration grows, you may focus on your opponent and the slow pace of play rather than on tennis. The slower your opponent plays, the more angry and distracted you become. Soon you are thinking about everything but your game and you can barely play.

Dealing with gamesmanship is tough because it triggers strong emotions. If you have a plan to handle these situations, you will find yourself managing better. The easiest way to

STRATEGY DRILL

Skill objective: Vary the direction of the ball by using a pattern
Psychological objective: Enhance focus

Procedure
1. Stand at the baseline.
2. Have a partner feed three balls to your forehand side.
3. Hit the first two balls crosscourt and the last ball down-the-line.
4. Repeat this drill with your backhand.

Options
1. Hit the first ball crosscourt and the last two balls down-the-line.
2. Have your partner feed you two deep balls and a short ball, put the short ball away.
3. Play a set where you use a set pattern every point.

develop a plan is to scout your opponents (see chapter 6 for more on scouting) so you will know if you are up against a notoriously slow player, a fast player, a line-call questioner, or a score forgetter. Once you know whom and what you are facing, you can mentally prepare yourself to handle the match calmly and effectively.

Slow tempo players. If you know that your opponent seems to do everything in slow motion, prepare. Practice playing at a slower tempo and have something to do while you are waiting for the points to begin. You may want to take some practice swings, adjust your strings, or bounce on your toes. Having a plan will help keep you relaxed and focused.

Speed demons. If your opponent's fast tempo of play is the problem, make sure that you take the time you need between points. Generally, you need a few seconds to think about what happened in the last point and a few seconds to prepare for the next point. Some people serve so fast that the ball is heading right at you while you are still thinking about the last point. In these cases, make sure that you are truly ready for the ball when you step into position to receive serve. If need be, turn your back on the server and take the time you need to mentally regroup. Remember, you are entitled to 25 seconds between points. If your opponent serves the ball when your back is turned, and you do not try to hit it, the point is considered a let and is replayed. If you do not turn away, are surprised by a quick serve, make a stab at the ball, and mishit it, you are considered ready (because you did hit the ball), and you lose the point. Turning around or stepping away gives you the extra time that you need.

Line-call doubters. Some players question their opponents' line calls as a form of gamesmanship. They try to intimidate you enough to make you hesitate to call balls out that are in fact out. Some players do this by asking "Are you sure?" when you call a ball out. Other players say "Oh yeah!" or "My point" (maybe even before the ball bounces) to let you know that they think that their shot was in. Don't let this form of gamesmanship work. The rules of tennis state that if a ball bounces on your side of the court, it is up to you to make the call. Call the lines to the best of your ability. Be honest, but be confident in your calls, too.

Score forgetters. It can happen any time in the match. All of a sudden, there is a disagreement about the score. It could be an honest mistake, or it could be a form of gamesmanship. That is, if your opponents "forget" the score and then remember it in their own favor, they are taking an unfair advantage (see *United States Tennis Association [USTA] Regulations* for score dispute regulations). Be prepared. Although it is the server's responsibility to say the score before each point, you may need to remind your opponent or to say it aloud yourself. If your match has long points and games, it can also be helpful to write the score on a piece of paper at changeovers or use score cards if they are available. Knowing the score will allow you to keep the points that you have won.

UNITED STATES TENNIS ASSOCIATION (USTA) REGULATIONS

Disputes over the score shall be resolved by using one of the following methods, which are listed in the order of preference:

• count all points and games agreed upon by the players and replay only the disputed points or games;
• play from a score mutually agreeable to the players;
• spin a racquet or toss a coin.

United States Tennis Association (1999). *Friend at court.* New York: United States Tennis Association, Inc., p. 80.

If you have the choice, avoid people who use gamesmanship. Gamesmanship can make tennis frustrating and take away from the fun of the game. If you have to play someone who resorts to gamesmanship tactics, prepare for the match, and you will find that this desperate attempt to win at all costs won't work against you.

Spectators

Tennis is played at public parks, schools, tennis clubs, and in stadiums. Even if you never play on center court, there are times when your matches will draw spectators. Knowing how to deal with fans (both your own and your opponents') will keep you playing your best when the pressure is on.

Your own fan club. Some people love having fans come to their matches. The extra support brings out their best tennis and adds fire to their shots. If you like crowd support, be sure to invite supporters to your matches. Both you and they will enjoy the game.

Some people find that having fans watch them play hurts their game. It may be the extra pressure or distraction that throws them off. Perhaps they worry about what their fans are thinking rather than what they are doing on the court. If people you know come to your matches, but you don't like having them watch you play, speak up. Explain the situation, and ask them to help you by not watching you play for a while. Feel free to be assertive about asking for tennis privacy, but don't banish spectators forever. Over time, you may find that your game has matured and that you play better and like the extra encouragement that supportive fans bring.

Other spectators. Playing an opponent who has fans can be intimidating. In some matches, your opponent's supporters are not just spectators, they are hecklers—criticizing line calls or cheering when you miss a shot. It is never easy to face this type of audience, but if you refocus, stay positive, or talk to tournament officials, you will be better able to keep yourself on track.

If you find you are getting mad at the spectators, then you are distracted. Knowing that you are distracted is the first step toward better play. Catch your breath, relax (see chapter 3 for more about relaxation), and prepare for the next point. By focusing on tennis, you may be able to mentally block out those fans.

If you've tried relaxing and focusing, but it is not enough, you may need to bring out some other mental tricks. Use positive self-talk (see chapter 13) to cheer yourself on. You can be as loud and enthusiastic in your mind as you want. Help yourself to get fired up to play. If it is hard for you to be positive, you might be able to use the energy from your opponent's fans to help. When you hear them cheer for your opponent, imagine that they are cheering for you. If they cheer after you miss a shot, think of it as encouragement to you for the next point. Doing this will help you smile to yourself every time the fans let out a roar and will help you keep your mind on your tennis, not on your frustration.

Summary

When you step out onto the court to play tennis, be prepared for highs and lows. Some matches will showcase your best play. Some matches will pit you against opponents who make questionable line calls, use gamesmanship, and have over-eager spectators. If you develop a plan and keep a sense of purpose, you will find that you are well equipped to overcome even the most difficult of these human challenges.

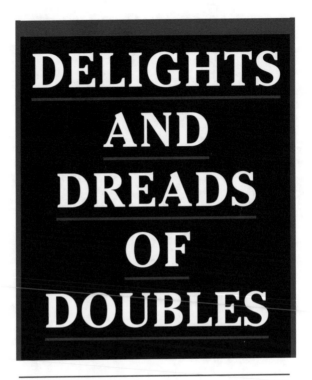

DELIGHTS AND DREADS OF DOUBLES

SECTION IV

HOW TO BECOME A TEAM

They seem totally comfortable together. They walk out on the court and know who is playing which side. They don't have to decide who will serve first. If one of them yells, "Yours," the other gets the ball. They high-five after good shots. They poach. They smile. You are playing your worst nightmare, a great doubles team.

Team Building

You can be part of a great doubles team, too, but you have to develop your teamwork. The first step is communication. I (CSB) know two average players who make an outstanding doubles team. As a team, they have won over 20 tournaments. Derek is the aggressive net specialist who hits tricky angles and has a killer overhead. Steve is the steady baseliner who runs down every shot. Through practice and competition they have learned to communicate constantly. They improve all the time because they also take tennis lessons to practice specific doubles drills, watch good doubles players (live and on TV), and have a team game plan.

Develop communication. Good communication lets two individual players think, move, and act as one. To improve doubles communication, work with your partner. Decide who will chase the lobs, who will handle the "down the middle" shots, and who will take the overheads. During points, make the "in" or "out" calls for the balls served to your partner. Also, practice cheering each other on and keeping each other informed by saying "yours," "mine," and "switch" when appropriate.

Janet and Marilyn were playing a league match when their opponents threw up a really annoying high lob. "Switch!" yelled Janet. Marilyn switched sides, chased down the lob, and won the point. One of their opponents came storming up to the net, "WHAT did you call me?" she demanded. It took a moment to sink in. Janet said, "Switch," but the opponent thought she'd heard a word beginning with the letter "b." Janet and Marilyn kept laughing the whole match and won it easily.

To get the best out of your on-court communication, you and your partner should talk about what helps each of you play better. For example, after a good shot, some people like the understated head nod "yes," whereas others like to high-five. It is especially important to discuss what to do if one of you is playing poorly. Some people find tennis tips help them regroup. If that works, a partner can serve as "coach" right on the court. Other people become even more frustrated if they are corrected. They feel as if they are being belittled, picked on, and not treated like equal members of the team. They might prefer to laugh it off. Tailor your response to your partner. Even your best joke won't help the situation if your partner is the quiet type.

You should talk about what you want your partner to say to you before you step on the tennis court (see *Team-Building Questions for Doubles* below for a list of useful questions). Try to think about what works and doesn't work for you. For example, I (JVR) have found that some phrases really bug me. "This game is really important" or "we need your first serve" makes me hit worse. Negative talk like "don't miss this return," "why did you hit that?" and "you missed it and we really needed that point" brings me, and indeed most people, down. Try to avoid the negative as much as possible. Positive

TEAM-BUILDING QUESTIONS FOR DOUBLES

Discuss these questions with your partner. Some possible answers to the questions are included below.

1. What would you like me to do when you make a mistake?
   a. Ignore it.
   b. Help me to laugh it off.
   c. Encourage me for the next shot.
   d. Remind me to use proper stroke mechanics.

2. What would you like me to do when the pressure is on?
   a. Nothing. Talking about pressure makes me more nervous.
   b. Remind me that it is a big point to help psych me up.
   c. Remind me to stay calm.

3. What would you like me to do when we are losing?
   a. Stay positive about our effort, to help me stay motivated.
   b. Communicate, so we can revise our strategy.
   c. Minimize communication; it makes me more frustrated.

4. How can I be a good partner?
   a. Keep your cool and stay motivated even if I make an error.
   b. Don't correct my strokes.
   c. Go for your shots no matter how I play.

5. How can we be a better team?
   a. Use more positive communication.
   b. Practice together on doubles drills.
   c. Compete together more.
   d. Have more fun.

statements like "I'm with you" or "nice get" are encouraging, helpful, and keep you and your partner playing your best. If you talk to your partner on a regular basis, you can modify your communication style as your team evolves.

Take doubles lessons. If you have found someone who makes a good partner, you can improve your doubles game by taking a lesson together. Let the tennis professional know that you want to work on doubles strategy and drills. This should be a team-building experience, not just a semiprivate lesson. You should learn to move together throughout the point and communicate so that you know who is going to hit each ball. Good doubles players hit the ball, not each other!

In top-notch doubles, the team that takes the net first typically wins the point (see *Team Net-Play Drill*, next page, for effective exercises). That's the position you want to be in. During your lesson, work on points where you serve and volley. Practice returning and coming into the net. Work on your overheads. Not everyone is comfortable at the net, but once you can get there in practice, you will be able to do it in a match.

In developing a doubles partnership, you and your partner need to decide which side of the court each of you will play. With right-handed players, if you have a big forehand and your partner has a killer backhand, it is easy to see who will play the deuce (forehand) and who will play the advantage (backhand) side. Most times, it is not that clear-cut. If need be, experiment during practice, or play one set in one position and switch for the next set. In general, the stronger of the two should play the advantage (backhand) side of the court. The best advice is to play the side that works for you and your team.

Watch good doubles. Whenever you have the chance to take in some good doubles, do it. Watch doubles on TV or, better yet, check it out live. Doubles is an exciting, fast-paced, action game. As you watch, be aware of the strategy and communication used. You will be able to pick up good competitive doubles ideas and a sense of excitement that will carry over into your own matches.

Develop a match plan. A good team has a strategy or match plan that works for them. Maybe the better server serves first

TEAM NET-PLAY DRILL

Skill objective: Move as a team and take the net
Psychological objective: Gain confidence as a doubles team

Procedure
1. One team stands at the baseline; the other team stands at the service line.
2. The team at the service line puts a ball into play and closes into the net.
3. The baseline team tries to win the point by passing or lobbing over the net team.
4. The net team tries to win the point by putting the ball away.
5. Play until one team gets 7 points and then switch team positions.

Options
1. The baseline team is not allowed to lob on the first shot.
2. Teams alternate position after each point.
3. The team that wins the point starts at the service line for the next point.

Tips
1. Work on communication with your partner during this drill (be sure to say "yours").
2. Be sure to get on balance (split step) before you volley.

in the set or the stronger player takes the balls down the middle. Perhaps one of the players hits lob returns of serve to catch the opponents out of position. Find what works for you as a team and stick with it.

For many teams, the match plan is slightly different for the stronger and weaker players. If you are the stronger player, you lead the team. Practice taking the shots down the middle or the balls that could be hit by either of you. Keep your favorite weapon and your confidence fired up. Remember to support your partner during the match. Cheer the good shots and provide encouragement after the missed balls. The best doubles teams communicate with and energize each other. The worst doubles teams have one player who hogs all the balls and another player who gets depressed.

If you are the weaker player, you can contribute to the team by using your strengths. Maybe you will lob the return of serve over the net person rather than smash winners. Maybe you will put the ball back in play and give your partner a chance to volley. Whatever your strengths are, stick with them. If you make a mistake, don't become caught up in apologizing. If you are committed to playing your best and if you keep trying, you will be the sort of partner that everyone wants to have.

Playing Doubles

You've worked on your communication skills, honed your net game, had your pregame talk with your partner, and developed a match plan. It is time to take on another doubles team. To play great doubles, try to scout your opponents prior to your match. Also make sure that you take the time to warm up before your match (see chapter 6 for more about warming up). If you warm up in advance, when your official warm-up begins, you'll be able to focus on your opponents' strengths and weaknesses instead of your own game.

Size up your opponents. As you warm up, do some on-court scouting and notice how your opponents play. Even if you have scouted your opponents earlier, you still need to pay attention. You want to learn how your opponents are playing today.

As you can see from the scouting report form (*Doubles Scouting Report on Chris and Terry,* next page), it is a good idea to hit your opponents some forehands, backhands, hard balls, soft balls, angle shots, volleys, and overheads. Try to identify each player's strengths and weaknesses. For example, the "ad side" player may love to hit hard backhands but could have trouble moving for short angled backhands or high topspin ones. Remember to check out volleys and overheads too. Some players have great ground strokes, but high lobs really throw them. These are the players to lob. If your opponents avoid certain types of shots during the warm-up—if they don't take any practice shots at the net, for example, they may be weak at the net. You'll have to wait and see.

During the warm-up period, you will probably practice some serves. Be sure that you take serves from both the advantage

DOUBLES SCOUTING REPORT ON CHRIS AND TERRY

1. *Name of opponents:* Chris and Terry
2. *Date of match:* August 3
3. *Score of match:* W 6–4, 6–3
4. *Court surface:* hard
5. *Weather conditions:* outdoors, hot and sunny

	Chris	Terry
6. *Handed:*	right	right
7. *Forehand:*	slices short balls	loads of topspin
8. *Backhand:*	short angles	topspin
9. *Forehand Volley:*	very strong	changes grip and misses sometimes
10. *Backhand Volley:*	has trouble with balls hit at body	decent, not a weapon
11. *Overheads:*	hates high lobs	solid
12. *Serves:*		
First:	topspin out wide	flat down middle
Second:	at the body	spin serve
13. *Movement:*	comes to net well	slow to short balls

14. *Movement as a team:* Don't move together as a team. When one player is out of position, the other does not cover.
15. *Style of play:* They serve and volley most of the time. Terry is sometimes slow to come in, and so they may be one up and one back. They are less aggressive when playing one up and one back.
16. *Best shot:* Both have really strong forehands.
17. *Weakest shot:* Chris's backhand volley, Terry's forehand volley.
18. *Suggested strategy:* Hit the ball right at their bodies when they come to net. Try not to lob. If you must lob, hit high balls to Chris. Hit short angles when possible to get them out of position.
19. *Other comments:* Be prepared for a competitive but fun match. Hang in there.

and deuce sides of the court so that you are ready to play when the match begins. Remember to notice how your opponents serve. Do they tend to serve down the middle, out wide, or right at your body? If you have the chance to return a few of their serves, take it. Returning will help you to develop a rhythm and know what to expect.

Once you have an overview of how your opponents play, figure out who is the overall weaker player. This is the person that you will hit to if things get rough. For example, I (CSB) was playing in a league match 2 years ago, and the other team had match point. I was returning serve on the backhand side. The serve came in to my forehand, and I drilled it right at the weaker player, despite the fact that he was at the net. Sure enough, he flubbed the volley, and we went on to win. Knowing where to hit the ball when you are in trouble is a big confidence booster.

During the warm-up, remember that your opponents are sizing you up, too. Stay positive even if you miss a shot— maybe they won't realize that it is your weakness. Communicate with your partner, stay loose, and you will set the tone for your match.

Either during or after the warm-up, talk to your partner. Share what you found out about your opponents. Tell your partner about a left-handed opponent (if there is one) and about the types of serves or ground strokes to expect. By jointly evaluating your opponents, you and your partner can develop a plan of attack and decide how you are going to play the match.

Reassess strategy during the match. In doubles, a basic strategy is the foundation of good play. Get to the net as much as you can. Hit the ball down the middle between your opponents. Use short angles. Lob or mix things up occasionally. Hit to the weaker player.

Depending on what you learn in warm-up, you may modify things a bit. If your opponents have shaky overheads, hit them plenty of lobs. If they like the ball hit hard, try hitting slice or softer, off-pace shots. Remember to continually assess your strategy throughout the match. For example, if the stronger player starts hitting winners from the weaker player's side of the court, stop hitting to the weaker player as much. Instead, hit out wide and catch the stronger player out of position.

When the stronger player misses shots it can confuse your opponents and undermine their team morale.

Dealing with the stronger player may be the biggest challenge of the match. One strategy is to try to force them to hit their weaker shots. If the stronger player has a big forehand, serve to the backhand. If they love short balls, keep the ball deep. Basically, players with killer shots love to use them. It's your job not to give them the opportunity.

Become a Team

You might think that practicing and competing together will make you a team. Sure, those are important steps, but for great doubles, you need even more. Create team chemistry, be a good partner, and there will be no stopping you.

Create team chemistry. For some teams chemistry just happens. You play together once, and you know that you've got "it." You are a team for the ages. For other teams, team chemistry evolves more slowly. You can help things along if you make the effort to become a team. So how do you become a team? The process will depend on your unique styles. You could drive to matches together and warm each other up or go out after a match for juice or other drinks. You could buy matching tennis shirts to wear when you compete. You might talk to each other on the telephone. Some great teams high-five each other after every good shot. Some teams use signals or have "inside" jokes. There's no one secret method. The important thing is to find what is fun and works for you. Knowing each other and caring about each other create a foundation for team chemistry. If you make the effort to develop it, you will find that good team chemistry will make your good matches great and will carry you through even when you are not playing your best.

Be a good partner. Team chemistry can't happen if one partner is always mad at the other. To be a team, both people have to pull their own weight and think of the good of the team. If you are a person who is chronically late, make an effort to be on time to team practices and matches. Take your turn bringing tennis balls. Make sure you have water. A doubles partnership is like any other relationship—work out the rough spots, communicate, and you will have wonderful tennis for lots of matches to come.

Call it quits when you have to. You can give your best effort and find that your doubles partner is not working out. With a good partnership, both players are important. Both contribute to the team. If you are steady and your partner is aggressive, then you both contribute. Maybe one of you brings the tennis balls, and the other brings the snacks. If both of you are happy, then that's a good partnership, too. Some doubles teams seem great in theory but don't work out in practice. Sometimes compatible players change. If the partnership is not working, move on. Find a new partner and begin developing a partnership so you will be back on the path to doubles fun.

Summary

Doubles is a fast-paced, exciting game that can really test your physical and mental skills. It is also a social game that can help you make a close friend. To enjoy doubles to its fullest, find a partner and become part of a team. Practice doubles strategy, communicate well, be positive, play matches together, and soon you will find yourself loving the game.

10

WHAT TO DO WHEN YOU CAN'T COUNT ON YOUR PARTNER'S GAME

YOU CAN DO IT!
I BELIEVE IN YOU!

You might have suspected it when your partner hit several wild shots in the warm-up. Maybe you figured it out when your partner's game fell completely apart in the first set. Whenever it happened, you thought to yourself, this is it. I'm out here playing doubles, and my partner just doesn't have it.

Play with a weak partner, and you could become frustrated. Play with a weak partner, and you could improve your tennis. Basically, it is up to you. If you want the best results when your partner's game is shaky, you must provide encouragement, keep playing doubles, and go for your shots (see *Help Your Partner Play Better*).

Provide Encouragement

When you are playing with a weak partner, provide a lot of encouragement. Let's face it, your partner needs it. After all, your partner is bound to feel bad. If you roll your eyes when your partner misses a shot or if you give too much advice, it is likely to make things worse. It may seem impossible that the situation could get worse, but it will. If you provide encouragement and enhance communication, you will be on your way to a better match.

HELP YOUR PARTNER PLAY BETTER

1. Support your partner if he or she tries to hit the right shot even if you lose the point (e.g., "it's good to return crosscourt," "good job coming to the net").
2. Have your partner help plan team strategy (be a team).
3. Stay positive.

Break the downward spiral. When people are playing badly, they know it. Even if they don't say anything, they are probably feeling nervous. The more nervous they get, the worse they play. The worse they play, the more nervous they get.

To break out of a downward spiral, you have to help your partner to feel better or hit better. To make your partner feel better (and less nervous), give encouragement. Even if your partner misses a shot, acknowledge the effort. You could say, "That was a good serve," even if the next shot was an error. You could say "Good job going for that volley" even if it was an easy put-away. If being really positive is awkward for you, or if your partner seems too frustrated, try another tactic. Smile or tell a joke. Making your partner laugh often helps. You can also try pointing out any problems that your opponents are having. For players on a bad day, misery loves company. Whatever you say, be sincere. With your support and enthusiasm, your partner will start playing better.

It is easy for us to *say*, "Be supportive," but with some partners it can be hard to *do*. Sometimes, you just can't believe how bad your partner is. We know that this happens, but even with a truly lousy partner, we suggest that you make the effort to hide your annoyance. Getting fed up with your partner only makes the situation worse. If you get mad, your partner will either give up and play worse or try really, really hard and probably play worse. In addition, if you yell at your partner, your opponents will know what is going on. You are mad. You are out of control. Your partner is nervous. Your opponents will probably hold a little party on their side of the court. By losing your cool, you make the match three players (you and your opponents) against one. Your poor partner is the one. Provide encouragement to stop the downward spiral, and you will have a much better match.

Keep Playing Doubles

When your partner is really weak, keep playing doubles. What else could you be playing? You could be playing half-baked singles. You see, some people, especially those who are frustrated with their partners, try to play singles on the doubles court. They go for every ball and dash around the court screaming "Mine!!" The problem is, this strategy doesn't work. If you have tried it, you know how painful it can be. Your opponents move the ball around to keep you zooming from side to side and to take advantage of the confusion on your side of the court. Your partner grows even more nervous and misses the few easy balls that come along. The whole match can go downhill fast. Keep playing doubles, keep things simple, protect team weaknesses, and you will be on your way to better tennis.

Keep things simple. Try to keep your plan of attack simple and capitalize on your strengths. When your partner is weak, don't try Australian doubles or the lob-drop shot combination. Instead, stick with high percentage doubles (see chapter 12) with a minor modification. The modification is that every ball that is down the middle or could be hit by either player is yours. You are the stronger player, so you take these shots. You also take the balls that are on your side of the court. Your partner hits only the balls that are on your partner's side of the court. When both you and your partner have divided the court and know where to be, you are on the way to better play.

Protect weaknesses. Sometimes you have a partner who isn't just weak. You have a partner who is truly, truly bad. This does not give you license to try to play singles on the doubles court. This does not give you license to give up. Keep playing doubles, but protect your team's weaknesses. How do you do that? First, you figure out what your team's biggest weakness is. Maybe your partner misses every single backhand. Have your partner play the forehand side and come in and volley. This strategy could help your partner avoid hitting backhands completely. Maybe your partner misses volleys. If so, have your partner stay in the back court. Be creative. Try hitting extra hard or try making your opponents run. If you throw your opponents off their usual game, they will probably hit more balls to you by mistake. By making changes to protect your team's weaknesses, you may surprise your opponents and even win some free points.

Go for It!

When your partner is weak, you are in an interesting position. You have no pressure. No one expects miracles from you. If you lose the match, it is because of your partner. If you win the match, you will be seen as a brilliant player. Sweet.

Lack of pressure is why playing with a shaky partner can be fun and good for your game. Take advantage of this situation.

GOAL SETTING

Set goals to improve your doubles play or other aspects of your game. Be as specific as possible when identifying your goals. The format below may be useful. For extra motivation, write your goals down and keep them with you.

Goal sheet #1

1. Skill/stroke Serve and volley

2. Specific goal Move to the net following serve

3. Measure of success Come to the net at least four times per service game

4. Strategy Serve a bucket of balls twice a week and practice running to the service line after each serve

5. Obstacles Lack of time and motivation

6. Overcome obstacles Fit in serving practice before regular tennis game to increase motivation and save an extra trip to the courts

Goal sheet #2

1. Skill/stroke Communication

2. Specific goal Communicate more to enhance teamwork

3. Measure of success Talk with my partner before every point

4. Strategy Discuss what I like to have my partner say during a match (and what my partner likes) and agree to increase communication

5. Obstacles Talking is awkward and possibly distracting

6. Overcome obstacles Keep communications brief, use most effective phrases

Remember, if a goal is not working for you, revise it. Setting clear goals and updating them periodically will bring out the best in your game.

Set goals and become a better doubles player (see *Goal Setting*). Poach. Go for the overheads. Try to serve and volley. Do the challenging things that you don't usually have the nerve to do to make your game better. If you practice these shots now, you will be able to use them in the future.

Summary

Playing doubles with a weak partner can be a challenge, but it can also be good for your game. If you communicate and work with your partner as a teammate, you will find that you can help your partner to play better. If you take advantage of the chance to go for your shots and practice some of the more challenging parts of your game, you will find that playing with a weak partner can be fun and rewarding.

WHAT TO DO WHEN YOU LET YOUR PARTNER DOWN

Ooh!

YIKES! I'm so SORRYEEE...

You wind up for a big serve, toss up the ball, and follow through. Smack! The ball hits the back of your partner's head. Your partner yelps and then gives you a look. Oops. Sorry. You're up at the net set up for a total put away shot. Your opponents are backing up on the other side of the court. Everyone is looking at you as *you go after the ball. You dash into position and swish. You miss the ball completely. Basically, there is no denying what everyone can see. You stink.*

It's tough when you have a bad day. There is nowhere to hide. You feel as if you are the worst player ever to step out on a tennis court. It may be because part of your game has left you. You just can't seem to hit your ground strokes. It may be you just look bad in comparison. You seem bad compared to the really good players you are playing with. In fact, the added pressure of trying to play like your strong opponents may make you hit worse than you usually do (see *Return of Serve Drill* for a drill to help handle big serves). Whatever it is that throws you off, you should know that there is hope. When your game abandons you, simplify, encourage yourself, stay ready, and work with your partner.

Simplify your Game

When your game is off, you are not going to be able to hit the fancy shots well. In fact, you may not hit anything well.

RETURN OF SERVE DRILL

Skill objective: Improve your return of serve
Psychological objective: Increase your confidence when returning strong serves

Procedure
1. Stand at the baseline, ready to receive serve.
2. Have a partner stand at the *service* line and serve the ball to you (this will make the serve come at you harder and faster).
3. Return the ball crosscourt.
4. Practice receiving from the other side.

Options
1. Have your partner vary the type of serve (flat, spin, slice).
2. Play out the point crosscourt with your partner.

Tips
1. Use a minimal backswing.
2. Have your partner serve slower paced balls to let you establish a rhythm.

That is frustrating. The good news is you can play the percentages and stick with the basics and find yourself on the way back to better play.

Play the percentages. Some shots are more likely to go in and win you the point than others are. These are the high-percentage shots. You will do much better if you play high-percentage tennis when your game is off. In doubles, the high-percentage serve is down the middle of the court. If you serve down the middle, your opponent will probably return back down the middle. Now your partner can go after the ball and hit a winning volley. When your game is off, it is nice to have your partner hit the ball.

When you are receiving serve or when you are volleying, the high-percentage shot is crosscourt. If you hit crosscourt, your shots will be more likely to stay in, and you will be hitting over the lowest part of the net. You can mix things up once in a while, but overall, crosscourt is the way to go (see *Crosscourt Consistency Drill* below).

CROSSCOURT CONSISTENCY DRILL

Skill objective: Hit returns of serve crosscourt consistently
Psychological objective: Stay focused while returning of serve

Procedure
1. Pretend you are playing doubles.
2. Hit all balls crosscourt.
3. Have a partner serve the ball to you.
4. If your crosscourt return of serve is good, you get 1 point.
5. Continue playing the point out.
6. The player who "wins" the rally also gets 1 point.
7. Play until one player reaches 11 points then switch servers.

Options
1. Serve and volley.
2. Return and volley.

Tips
1. Say the score aloud before each serve.
2. The scoring system gets easier after you play a few points.

Good advice, you say, but you know that on bad days, you can't volley crosscourt because you can't make it to the net. In fact, you are stuck in the back court faced with two opponents at the net. Keep up the high-percentage tennis. If you are back and your opponents are both up at net, the high-percentage shot is the classic down-the-middle ball. Hit right between your opponents, and you have the benefit of hitting the ball over the lowest part of the net. If your opponents are not that good as a team, they may be confused about whose ball it is and either let it go or crash racquets both trying to volley. Either scenario makes them look bad and takes the attention off you. When you are struggling like this, it is nice to have company.

Stick with the basics. If you are playing badly, you may start feeling depressed or frustrated. The worse you feel, the more you try unusual shots such as the down-the-line service return winner or the drop shot. Resist the urge. Stick with the basics. Sticking with the basics means letting your partner know that you are not going to take the "anyone's" balls. Go for your shots, but leave the high overheads and other difficult shots for your partner.

Sticking with the basics also means watching the ball and getting your feet moving. If you see the ball and are in position, you will hit better. Take little running steps, keep your eye on the ball, and you will find that your game is improving.

Encourage Yourself

You are trying to play high-percentage tennis and to move your feet. You are trying. Then you look up and notice your partner sighing because you missed a ball, or maybe you see your opponents smirking. What do you do? There are a lot of things that you feel like doing, but these will probably hurt your game. Try to stay positive and encourage yourself and you will have a fighting chance.

Stay positive and confident. Get positive and stay there. If you lose a point, it is not the end of the world, it is not even the end of the match—it is just one point. If your opponent hits a good shot and wins the point, give credit where credit is due.

It was not your error; it was simply a good shot. Cheer yourself on. If you tried, acknowledge the effort and praise yourself. Think "good try." It can be hard to be sincere when you are playing pathetically, but do your best. If truly being positive is beyond you, fake it. Pretend that you are having fun, that you like yourself and enjoy tennis. You will probably fool your opponents, who will start to worry about when you are going to "turn it on." You may even fool yourself and start playing your game again!

Don't encourage the other team by "dissing" yourself. When you yell at yourself and look mad, you send the other team a clear message. They know that you are losing it. This makes your opponents happy. They know that they can take advantage of the situation and win the match even faster. If you become so mad that you need to blow off steam, turn around so that the other team can't see you. That way, it will look like as if you are thinking and are under control. On a bad day, you have enough problems. Don't help the other team out.

Stay Ready

When you are playing lousy tennis, you are probably going to be hitting a lot of balls. That's because your opponents have noticed that your game is weak today. They are going to hit the ball to you as much as they can. You can become frustrated or you can be fired up to play. After all, knowing the other team's strategy is an advantage. You can be ready for their shots before they come. You may even find that hitting lots of balls helps you recover your rhythm. Stay ready and you may be able to turn this match around.

Communicate With Your Partner

When you are having a bad day, it can be tough on both you and your partner. You may find yourself apologizing to your partner for your shots. Remember, your partner knows that you did not miss that ball on purpose. By apologizing, you are reminding your partner that your game is off. This will not make your partner feel any better. In fact, it will probably make them disappointed or aggravated. It will also make you feel worse. That is not good. What should you do? Here are two ideas. First, tell your partner that you know that your game is off. Explain that you are trying to stay positive and focused for the team, but if there is anything else you can do, you will surely try it. Second, ask what your partner needs from you. How can you help out? Not too much advice, but a simple tip might really help. If you keep your head in the game, and keep your partner feeling good, you will have a chance to get back in the thick of it.

Summary

It is no fun to be the tennis player who is playing badly. It is even worse when you are playing doubles and several other people are affected. There is no miracle cure for poor tennis play, but there are several steps you can take. Simplify your game, provide encouragement for yourself, stay ready, communicate with your partner, and you will find that you have made the best of a tough situation.

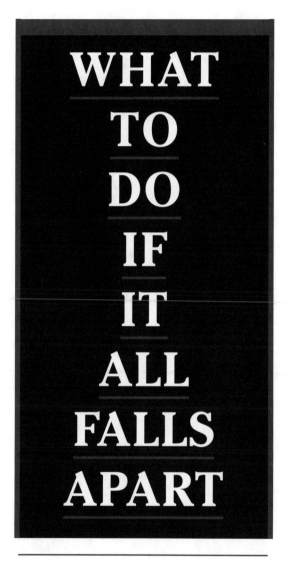

WHAT TO DO IF IT ALL FALLS APART

SECTION V

HOW TO RECOVER YOUR TENNIS STROKES

Sometimes it happens after you've taken some time off from tennis. Sometimes it surprises you after you've been playing great. All of a sudden you can't hit the ball in the court, or you can't serve, or your backhand has deserted you. What has happened to your game? Where is your game? Most important, how can you get your game back? HELP!

When your game falls apart, it can feel as if you will never be able to hit a real tennis shot again. I (CSB) remember vividly when it happened to me. I lost my serve during a close second-set match in a big tournament. I usually win my serve. On my next service game, I concentrated twice as hard to be sure to win. I began thinking too much and lost my serve again, double faulting twice. My next time around, I decided to change strategies. I altered my serve technique and didn't win a point. I had no feel, no rhythm, and no game. If this happens to you, don't despair. Don't give up tennis and take up golf. What you need is a refresher course in the tennis basics.

The tennis basics come in two flavors: mental and physical. It's a sort of mind and body connection thing. You can start on the physical side of your game (keep reading this chapter), and the mental end will come along; or you can start on the mental part (see chapter 13), and the physical will follow. Actually, if you work on both mental *and* physical tennis basics, your entire game will benefit.

The physical basics are watching the ball, following through, and using proper footwork. If your game has gotten completely out of whack (or parts of it were never quite "in whack"), then this chapter should help. Putting in the time on the basics will pay off for you in terms of greater consistency and more fun.

Watch the Ball

In tennis you can win the point even if you hit the ball off the racquet frame. Granted, you bought the whole racquet, so you might as well use it all when you play. We have found, however, that if you hit the balls with the strings, and out in front of you, you will have more tennis success.

If you keep missing the ball, it is possible that you are not really watching it when you hit. Often, what you are watching is your opponent or the open court where you are going to hit the ball. Concentrate on the ball (see *Decision Drill*, next page). Some people watch the ball actually make contact with their racquet. Some people even say that they watch the ball so closely that they can see it spin or read the writing on it. If you can't see the ball that clearly, that's OK. You will still benefit from trying to watch the ball. You will find that focusing on the ball helps you to move into the right position to hit. When your game is off, watch the ball extra hard as you hit, and you will start concentrating and playing better.

DECISION DRILL

Skill objective: Watch the ball better
Psychological objective: Improve quick decision making

Procedure
1. Stand at the baseline.
2. Have a partner feed three balls to your forehand side.
3. As the ball crosses the net, your partner yells out "crosscourt" or "down-the-line."
4. Hit the ball where directed.
5. Repeat this drill with your backhand.

Options
1. Have your partner yell the direction just before the ball bounces.
2. Have your partner feed you balls anywhere in the court.

Follow Through

When you are slightly off your game, you hit more balls out of the court than usual. What often happens is that when you try to shorten your swing to keep more balls in, you find that you are hitting more balls out. Why this frustrating paradox? When you change your swing, you stop following through all the way. The follow-through is what puts spin on the ball and helps control where the ball is going. You need your follow-through. If you notice that you are hitting balls out, try accelerating the racquet head as you hit. The increased racquet-head speed on a follow-through that goes from low to high actually keeps balls in.

Focus on Footwork

The best tennis strokes in the world are little help if you don't reach the ball in time to use them. In tennis, you have to both run and hit the ball. Don't let poor footwork kill your game.

When you are running for a ball, make sure you go after every shot and use little steps to get into position.

FOOTWORK AND POSITIONING DRILL

Skill objective: Improve your ground stroke footwork and positioning
Psychological objective: Enhance confidence
Procedure
1. Identify your stronger ground stroke (forehand or backhand).
2. Find two targets (small cones, tennis ball can lids, racquet covers).
3. Create the boundaries of a center of the court "alley" by placing the targets 7 feet apart and 7 feet in front of the baseline.
4. Have your partner hit balls to you down the middle of the court, between the targets.
5. Move into position to hit *every* ball with your stronger ground stroke.
Options
1. Return all balls crosscourt or down-the-line.
2. Alternate returns, one crosscourt and one down-the-line.

Get to the ball. In tennis, you have to run for the ball. If the ball goes over the net, it is yours. Don't wait for an invitation to start running. Take the shortest diagonal path to every shot. If your opponent tends to hit to one spot, cheat over in that direction (see *footwork and positioning drill* above). Anticipate where your opponent will hit if possible and start moving as soon as you can. Expecting to hit lots of balls and practicing running down lots of balls will start you on the path to solid footwork.

Take little steps. Reaching the general vicinity of the ball is good, but it is not enough. You need to be in the proper position to hit, not too far away and not too close to the ball. If you take giant running steps, you will find yourself using wacky swings to compensate for your poor position. You might even miss the ball completely. Instead of elephant steps, try to take quick, little steps to speed yourself to the ball. You will find that taking small steps helps you to adjust to unusual spins, bad bounces, and pace and still lets you set up to hit.

Summary

There are times when you are out on the tennis court and you just don't have it. You can recover your game if you watch the ball, follow through, and get your feet into position. We know that this sounds simple, but you will find that working on these physical tennis basics will start your game on the road to recovery. As a bonus, using the basics will give your game improved consistency and control.

13

HOW TO REVIVE YOUR MENTAL GAME

Sometimes things happen that throw you off your game completely. My dad (JVR) was playing a match when his opponent threw up a high lob. Dad looked at the ball, lined up for the overhead, swung, hit his shin, and fell on the ground; the ball came down and bounced on his head. All dignity was lost. At an indoor tournament match, a top-ranked junior player, Jonathan C., lost his temper after missing a shot and flung his racquet toward the ceiling. The racquet got stuck up in the lights. Oops.

POING!

yuk yuk!

Even when you are hitting well, circumstances can throw you off. That's why the mental side of the game is so important. If you want to improve the mental side of your tennis game, you are going to have to go for it, toe the line, bite the bullet, and realize that you are going to need to use every positive cliché that you can think of to help carry you through the frustration of bad days. When you have lost it, you can get it back and even improve your game by being patient, being relaxed, being positive, using visualization, using routines, and letting your game happen.

Be Patient

When your game has taken a lunch break, you might be tempted to smack shots extra hard. Although this can be fun, it usually won't help you return to your winning game. That's because even if you win some glorious points, the majority of the balls are likely to go flying out. Instead, stay in the point for a while, maybe even longer than usual. If you have lost your temper, take a deep breath, settle down, and be patient.

Being patient does not mean that you have to be a tennis wimp. Go with your strengths. If you like to crush short balls, you can still do it. Patience for you means wait until you get a short ball. Don't smack the deep ones. If you are usually a steady player, use that aspect of your game. If you can't seem to be consistent, simplify. Hit the ball over the net right down the center of the court. If it won't go over the net, think to yourself, "Stick with it. Just hit it higher over the net." Whatever your approach, give yourself time to get it right. You will be amazed how much better you do when you are a patient player (see *Patience Drill* on page 109).

Relax

This is only a tennis match that you are playing. If you can keep your perspective when your game is off, you will feel better and play better tennis. That's because when you are tense and frustrated, your arm is tight and your strokes suffer. What you need to do is relax. Take a few deep breaths (see chapter 5 for more about relaxing) and regroup. If you know any jokes to tell yourself, now would be the time to use them. Sure, you look a little strange chuckling alone on your side of the court, but you are much more relaxed when you are laughing. Who knows? It might throw your opponent off a bit too. Remember, you like to play tennis: Breathe, relax, and give it your best shot.

RUBBER BAND REMINDER

Psychological objective: Reduce use of negative self-talk

Procedure
1. Put a rubber band on your wrist during a tennis practice.
2. Every time you think or say a negative self-statement, snap the rubber band on your wrist.
3. Try to reduce the number of rubber band snaps.

Option
1. Use the rubber band technique during a match.

Use Positive Self-Talk

When your game is off, you are often the first one to notice. Your opponent may think that you missed just one shot, but you are thinking that you will never hit a decent backhand as long as you live. You can tell yourself just how pathetic you are, but that won't help you play or feel better. Give yourself a break (see *Rubber Band Reminder* to help eliminate negative self-talk). Frankly, at this point, you need all the help you can get. Give yourself encouragement to keep trying and credit for what you are doing right (see *Positive Self-Talk Statements,* next page). Think of yourself as your own coach. A good coach would encourage you to keep trying and would notice good things about your game, even on a bad day. Treat yourself as a good coach would so you can feel and play better.

POSITIVE SELF-TALK STATEMENTS

Try using these self-talk statements when you are playing. Add to the list with phrases that work well for you.

Good hustle!

Good strategy idea.

Go for it!

Put the pressure on.

I can do it!

Way to keep fighting.

They are tough, but I am tougher.

Visualize

You can give yourself some extra on-court help if, in your mind, you go over the shots you want to improve (see chapter 6 for more about visualization). If your forehand is making you crazy, picture yourself hitting the forehand the way that you want to. Imagine it in slow motion, and you will have extra time to mentally perfect the shot. Some people find that it helps to hold their tennis racquets and take practice swings as they imagine the proper stroke. Visualization allows you to gain free practice time in the middle of your match. It can also let you spot problems and fix them before you mess up more points. Use the time between points or during changeovers for visualizing, and your game will be back on track sooner.

Use Routines

Routines are behaviors that you do every time you play. You may take a deep breath and bounce the ball twice before you serve. You may adjust your racquet strings and jump on your toes before you return serve. When your game is not going well, there is the tendency to rush though the points and skip your regular routines. Resist! Slow down! Your routine is a good friend. Routines keep you on target when you are playing well and can help you get going again when your game is off.

Let It Happen

It is good to have an arsenal of physical and mental remedies for times when your game is off. Use any strategy or combination of strategies to help you out on your bad days. If you use a hundred things at once, though, you will overload and end up even more annoyed—the dreaded paralysis by analysis. The simplest approach is often best. Try what you can. See what works. If your usual solutions aren't helping, don't panic, don't overanalyze, and don't get mad. Just play!

PATIENCE DRILL

Skill objective: Hit the ball consistently
Psychological objective: Play patiently during long points

Procedure
1. Stand at the baseline.
2. Hit balls down the middle of the court to your partner.
3. Count each shot as you rally.
4. Work with your partner to hit as many balls in a row as you can.

Options
1. Try to hit your shots deeper than the service line.
2. Start the rally with slow shots and increase the pace throughout the rally.

Summary

We all have days when we can't seem to play. All of us. When you seem to have lost it in the biggest way, there are several steps you can take. Refocus on the mental basics: Relax; be patient; be positive. Incorporate visualization and routines into your game, and you will find that you are playing better on the good days and holding your own on the off days.

GETTING (AND STAYING) IN THE GAME

SECTION VI

HOW TO GET STARTED IN TENNIS

Someone's probably said to you, "Tennis—that seems like fun." Or maybe it is your child, or a friend, or your spouse who wants to get started in the game. You agree that tennis is a great game, but how can they become involved?

Tennis has many things going for it. It helps you stay in shape, spend time with friends, and compete. Tennis is a sport you can play for a lifetime. USA Tournament Tennis includes competition for people ranging in age from 12 and under to 85 and over. You can play as long as you can walk. If you aren't ambulatory, you can play wheelchair tennis. Tennis, literally, has something for everyone. OK, so you're convinced that tennis is worth trying. Your questions now are "How do I begin?" "When should I begin?" and "What equipment do I need?"

How to Begin

The best way to start in tennis is just to go out there and give it a try. USA Tennis has a number of programs (e.g., USA Tennis Free For All) designed to get people started. These programs are fun and free. Find more information by contacting your local tennis club, tennis professional, or the United States Tennis Association (see *Where to Find Tennis Instruction Information* below).

If you want to try tennis on a less formal basis, hit with a family member or friend who knows how to play (see *Five Ways to Support a New Player,* next page, for tips). Be warned, however, that this approach can be frustrating. You may spend much of your time picking up balls, getting unsolicited advice, and feeling aggravated or embarrassed.

Group lessons are a great way to learn the basics of tennis. If you take some lessons, you will also meet people of similar

WHERE TO FIND TENNIS INSTRUCTION INFORMATION

*United States Tennis Association (USTA):
national headquarters (914) 696-7000
www.usta.com

*United States Professional Tennis Association (USPTA):
1-800-877-8248
www.uspta.org

*United States Professional Tennis Registry (USPTR):
1-800-421-6289
www.usptr.org

ability to practice with outside of class. USA Tennis 1-2-3 has a structured curriculum consisting of six 1 1/2 hour sessions for both adults and children. Lessons include forehands, backhands, volleys, serves, strategy, communication, and scorekeeping. By the last session, you will be ready to play a doubles match with your classmates. Upon graduation from this course, you might want to join USA Team Tennis (for adults and children) and participate in organized, supervised doubles competition in a round-robin format.

When to Begin

There is no perfect age to start tennis. Some top players had tennis balls hanging from mobiles in their cribs. Some didn't pick up the game until their early teens. Most elite players started playing somewhere between those two extremes. In general, the best time to start is when a child is old enough to follow simple directions and is able to stay interested in one activity for at least half an hour.

If you are no longer a child, it is not too late for you to start. All you need is some interest, motivation, and basic equipment (see *Tennis Equipment Basics,* next page).

Equipment

Tennis racquets. You can dust off the cobwebs from a friend's racquet to get started, but you may be better served by buying a new racquet of your own. Tennis racquet technology has undergone significant changes in the last several years. New racquets offer improved playability and reduce the likelihood

FIVE WAYS TO SUPPORT A NEW PLAYER

1. Support the newcomer's tennis goals.
2. Focus on effort not outcome.
3. Be positive.
4. Be helpful, but don't overdo it.
5. Leave the teaching to the professionals.

of injuries. You can buy a basic racquet for about $25 (junior racquet for about $15) at a discount store. As your game advances, move up in terms of racquet performance. Tennis specialty shops and tennis clubs often have "demo" racquets that you can try. *Tennis* magazine publishes reviews of new racquets on a yearly basis describing the type of game and level of player that each racquet is ideal for.

Courts. Most towns have public courts available for free or a minimal fee. You may also find free courts at high schools and colleges in your area. If you can find time to play only at night, look for courts with lights. You can also play indoors. Check your local yellow pages under Tennis Courts or Tennis Clubs.

Balls. There are tennis balls specifically designed for play on clay, play on hard courts, and even for practice play. Select balls that match your playing surface. Buy new balls regularly.

Tennis shoes. Do not wear running shoes to play tennis. They are not designed for side-to-side movement. Tennis shoes, court shoes, and even cross-trainers give you better support.

TENNIS EQUIPMENT BASICS

To get started in tennis you need
- Racquet
- Tennis balls
- Tennis shoes
- Court to play on

How to Keep Improving

The basics are a good beginning. However, you may want to improve your tennis more so that you can play on a high school or college team, in a league, or with family and friends. Consider taking private lessons with a reputable tennis professional. If you have a tennis friend of similar ability, you can take semiprivate lessons at half the cost. Your tennis professional may also have suggestions of hitting partners for you.

If you don't have someone to hit with, you can use a backboard or a ball machine. This type of practice helps you develop consistent strokes. If you have the court to yourself, get a bucket of balls and practice your serve.

Competition is an important way to improve your tennis. Play sets with a practice partner. Participate in a club tennis ladder, or join an interclub team. If you enjoy being part of a team, USA League Tennis offers ability-matched team competition for adult players. USA Tournament Tennis sanctions tournaments for adults and children by age-group and ability. For more information about USA Tennis programs, contact the United States Tennis Association (see *Where to Find Tennis Instruction Information*).

Improving the mental side of tennis is also important to your game. Remember to be patient with yourself as you learn new skills. Spend time practicing psychological techniques, such as imagery (see *Deep Slow Breathing* in Chapter 3) and relaxation (see *Visualization* in Chapter 6).

15

GETTING AND STAYING PHYSICALLY FIT

It could happen right in the middle of a point. You line up to hit a great shot and then—"ouch!" You feel a sharp, intense pain. Sometimes it's not so dramatic; you just start to notice a nagging ache that doesn't seem to go away. However it happens, you don't need anyone to tell you that injuries are the worst.

Even the best players on the planet get injured. You can prevent many injuries by being in good shape. If you do get injured, seek medical care. In addition, you can use imagery, goal setting, and patience to facilitate your recovery. There are specific steps you can take to help recover from the typical tennis problems of blisters, sore muscles, tennis elbow, and rotator-cuff tears (see *Five Steps to Better Injury Rehabilitation*). Knowing how to deal with tennis injury will help you get back out on the court where you belong.

FIVE STEPS TO BETTER INJURY REHABILITATION

1. Consult your doctor (a sports medicine professional if possible).
2. Learn about your injury. Find out what caused it and if there is anything you can do to prevent recurrence.
3. Ask specific questions about how long the doctor expects your recovery to take.
4. Ask what you can do to recover faster (e.g., rest, ice, specific exercises, medication).
5. Follow the doctor's instructions. Use goal setting (see *Goal Setting* in chapter 10) to help carry you through your rehabilitation.

Get in Shape

Tennis is a physically demanding sport. Sure, you can vary the amount of energy needed to play by choosing your opponent and the format, but don't be fooled. Although singles usually involves significant running, you can also work up a good sweat playing doubles.

Getting in shape is the best way to avoid injuries. Although detailed analysis of physical training is beyond the scope of this book, we recommend that you follow a thorough medical checkup with regular aerobic conditioning, stretching, and weight training. Aerobic work includes running, cycling, swimming, or aerobics classes. You want to work on endurance (e.g., running about 2 miles at a stretch is a solid base) and speed (e.g., short sprints). Stretching for 10 to 15 minutes on the court before or after you play will increase your flexibility and agility. Weight training with free weights or machines will increase your strength. If you need assistance expanding your fitness regimen, consult a fitness expert. Any steps you make toward better physical fitness will help your current game and keep you playing healthy longer (see *Five Ways to Find the Motivation and Time to Get in Shape*).

Before you play tennis, you should be physically ready. We're not saying that you have to be as fit as a professional athlete;

FIVE WAYS TO FIND THE MOTIVATION AND TIME TO GET IN SHAPE

1. Make fitness a priority.
   — Include running and/or weight training on your "to do" list and you will find a way to fit it in.
   — Schedule fitness workouts in advance. Otherwise you will find that you are "too busy" to work out.

2. Remember why you are getting in shape.
   — Scheduling 30–60 minutes a day for yourself will make you healthier, happier, and a better performer in all areas of your life (including tennis).
   — When you are in shape, you will have more energy for all your activities.

3. Create a "basic workout" of just 15 minutes.
   — On days that you can't do a full workout, squeeze in your basic workout to help you stay on the fitness track.
   — It doesn't matter what the workout is—running, biking, weights, stretching, walking, as long is it is ready when you need it. You **will** need it.

4. Use your "free time" to exercise.
   — Use exercise as transportation—run, bike, or walk to work or school.
   — Stretch or use exercise equipment while watching TV.

5. Find balance.
   — Don't overload your fitness training when you have tennis competition coming up or extra pressure at home, work, or school.
   — If fitness training goes up, make sure the other pressures in your life go back down.

we're just saying that the more physical energy you have, the easier it is to be mentally tough. When you are in shape, the focus of your game will be your new strategy or your volley, not your aching back (or tired legs or sore shoulder).

Stay in the Game Mentally

Being injured and having to leave the game for a time can be tough. You may grow frustrated waiting and try to come back too soon. Before you reinjure yourself, realize that using goal setting and imagery will help keep your tennis game sharp while giving you the time that you need to heal.

Goal setting. It can feel like forever when you are waiting to recover so you can return to tennis. Even the progress that you make can seem as if it is "not enough." You may feel like giving up completely. Don't despair and don't give up. Goal setting is the perfect technique for motivating you to get back out to the tennis courts.

Your sports medicine professional can help you come up with realistic recovery goals. If treating this injury yourself, think carefully about what has happened in the past. How long did it take you to recover from other injuries? Did you take enough time off to heal, or did you return to tennis too soon and reinjure yourself? Be honest with yourself so you can set appropriate, specific, measurable goals for your recovery.

Probably the most important thing for you to do is set specific goals. These goals might include using ice on a sore area for 20 minutes, stretching for 10 minutes, and imaging before you go to bed. You might set a "time off" goal where you take a week (more or less, depending on your injury) off from all activities to give yourself a chance to heal.

Set goals and reassess them regularly. Reward yourself as you meet your goals, or revise them so you can meet them in the future. If you follow a goal-setting program, you will soon feel the joy of making progress towards recovery.

Imagery. So you can't go out on the court to play. That's a shame, but you can still stay in the game by using imagery. Imagery is probably something that you already do. It is imagining yourself playing tennis. When you are injured you may have some extra time to use imagery. Take advantage of it. You can visualize yourself hitting a particular shot, maybe your backhand. You can imagine yourself hitting from both external and internal imagery perspectives. External imagery is seeing yourself from the outside, as if you are watching yourself on video. Internal imagery is feeling yourself actually hitting the shot. Don't confine yourself to individual strokes. You can go over whole points, games, and even matches in your head. You could imagine your arch-rival, favorite opponent, or Wimbledon champion. Practicing tennis in your mind will help you play better when you return to the court.

Imagery can also help in the healing process. You can imagine your injured body part getting stronger, the white blood cells rushing to the area and repairing the damage. Research has shown that healing imagery speeds recovery from injury. This may sound flaky, but it's worth a try. After all, it could help you to get back out on the court sooner!

Patience. The hardest thing to do when you are injured is be patient. I (JVR) learned exactly how hard it is to be patient when I tore my anterior cruciate ligament (ACL) playing doubles. First, I had to wait for the swelling in my knee to go down. Then I had knee surgery and a 6-month rehabilitation period. The whole experience was painful and frustrating.

Remember that a physical setback is not the end of the world or of your tennis game. Hang in there and be your own cheerleader. When you return to the game, you will find that it comes back to you. It's like riding a bicycle: It will take some time to recover all your skills, but you won't forget how to play.

Common Tennis Injuries

Even if you are in the best shape of your life, it is still possible for you to get injured playing tennis. Luckily, you are probably vulnerable to only a few of the most common tennis injuries. For example, some people never suffer from blisters, but have a problem with tennis elbow. Other people have muscle aches, but their shoulders feel great. Think about the injuries that you (or your close family members) have had in the past. These are the ones that you will want to take extra care to avoid.

If you are injured, you should seek medical assistance. After you go to the doctor, remember to follow the advice you are given. It is amazing how often people spend their time and money for medical help and then ignore what they have been told. For you to play at your best, you are going to have to find medical professionals whom you trust and then do what they suggest. This may involve taking time off, using ice regularly, or doing special exercises. All of these activities will help you recover. It seems obvious that you should follow the doctor's orders to heal properly, but so many people ignore advice that they do not like that we thought we should say something about it.

Blisters. Rubbing causes blisters. You can get blisters on your feet if your shoes don't fit properly or if your feet sweat and rub against your socks. Blisters aren't serious, but they hurt. Prevent foot blisters by wearing tennis shoes that fit. Wear good athletic socks that absorb sweat, and if you need extra help, powder your feet before you put on your socks and shoes.

So what do you do if it is too late to prevent the blister and you have a big one? If the blister has popped, keep the area clean and dry. You can wash the area, put on a Band-Aid, and keep on playing. If the blister hasn't popped and the match must go on, cushion the area with a gel layer to take away the painful pressure. You can buy gel products at any drugstore. If you are blister prone, keep some gel in your tennis bag. Eventually your blisters will turn to calluses, and this problem will be solved.

Sore muscles. Your muscles might feel sore after your first day out on the courts, after a hard practice, or after a long match. You may not feel sore until the day after you've played hard. Whenever you feel it, sore muscles are a real pain.

When your muscles are sore, the best thing to do is ice them. Sure, a nice warm heating pad sounds as if it would feel better than ice, but ice helps decrease inflammation and speeds healing. To ice an injury, put ice in a bag, wrap it in a towel, and put it on the sore part. Put the ice pack on for 20 minutes, then take it off for 20 minutes; put it on for 20 minutes, then take it off for 20 minutes. Two cycles of on/off is usually enough. If you are still in pain, try more cycles and consider consulting a medical professional. We know ice is cold, but for your aching muscles, ice is nice.

In addition to ice, you can take over-the-counter anti-inflammatories and do some gentle stretching. You can also massage the sore area. You can massage yourself, but better yet, find yourself a willing masseuse.

If you keep suffering from sore muscles, use ice, stretching, and massage, but also take a serious look at your game. If you are continually sore, then you may be overstressing your muscles. It could be that you are hitting the ball incorrectly, or maybe certain muscles are weak. Consult a tennis professional and a sports medicine specialist, and you will be on your way to less muscle pain.

Tennis elbow. Tennis elbow is soreness in your racquet arm near the elbow. If you have it, you don't need us to tell you about it—you know it hurts.

When you put too much stress on the muscle in your forearm, you start down the road to tennis elbow. It begins with a sore spot at the outside of the elbow where the muscle meets the bone. Many people with tennis elbow feel a sharp pain when they hit the ball. If you are vulnerable to tennis elbow, you have probably found that it hurts more when you're playing a lot of tennis. Tennis elbow can worsen if you use a racquet grip that is too big or if you hit incorrectly for extra spin.

There are several ways to prevent tennis elbow. First, check to see that your racquet grip is the right size. Hold the racquet as if you are ready to hit a forehand and look at the open space between your index (pointer) finger and the bottom of your thumb. The index finger of your other hand should be able to fit in that space. If there is too much space, try a smaller grip; if there is not enough space, try a bigger grip. Even though it takes a little while to become comfortable with a new grip, using the right grip size will cut down the stress on your forearm and will help with your tennis elbow pain. Second, try re-stringing your racquet at a lower string tension. Looser strings will decrease the shock that is transmitted from the racquet to your arm. Third, work on your swing technique. Take a lesson with a knowledgeable tennis professional and learn to swing correctly. You will hit the ball better and also gain long-term pain relief. We understand that these solutions require major tennis changes on your part. But if you have serious tennis elbow, you know that it is worth it to go the extra mile to play without constant elbow aggravation.

Maybe you are not yet ready for our earlier suggestions, or maybe you have already tried them and are ready for more ideas. You could try using a vibration dampener. There are a number of gizmos on the market that go on the strings and re-duce racquet (and elbow) vibration. You might want to try wearing an elbow-band brace. These braces are designed to re-duce the stress on your sore elbow. They don't solve the un-derlying problem, but they might make you feel better. Some people swear by elbow braces; others find that they do not make much difference. If you are in significant pain, you may want to try a brace and see if it works. You should also consult a sports medicine professional. Medical advice might include doing specific stretching and strengthening exercises for your tennis muscles as well as taking aspirin (or other anti-inflam-matories) and using ice to promote healing. Finally, if you have big tennis-elbow problems, you have probably heard from someone who doesn't play tennis that to prevent tennis elbow, you simply stop playing tennis. We think that this is lousy ad-vice. Stop playing tennis, no! If things are really bad, find a rac-quet with the right-size grip, take some lessons, and consult with a sports medicine professional. If all else fails, we say learn to play with your other hand!

Rotator cuff. Inside your shoulder is your rotator cuff. The rotator cuff is actually five muscles around your shoulder that work together to allow you to serve, hit overheads, and do other wonderful things. Many rotator-cuff injuries are overuse injuries. Sure, some people can play a lot of tennis and never have any shoulder problems, but for vulnerable players, problems generally occur when they learn a new stroke or start playing more than usual. To prevent and take care of rotator-cuff injuries, you should warm up before you play, use good stroke and serve technique, and use a light racquet. If you have shoulder pain that wakes you up at night, things are serious. Go to a sports medicine professional and have your shoulder checked out.

Summary

If you can avoid injury altogether, do it. Getting in shape and knowing your vulnerabilities will help you prevent common tennis injuries. If you are hurt, minimize the damage. Use goal setting, imagery, patience, and good medical advice to recover fast. Once you are better, continue with your goal setting, stretching, and other fitness plans to prevent injuries in the future. It isn't fun to be hurt, but doing these things will get you back out on the court and keep you out there playing.

AFTERWORD

In a one-mile race, the person who is fastest usually wins. The beauty of tennis is that good mental skills can win a match for a player who is not the fastest or most technically gifted.

How can you cope with playing retrievers, the players who drive most people nuts? How can you successfully challenge the club champion? How can you play well on those crucial big points and in the big matches? The answers to these questions are at the tip of your fingers.

Read (or reread) the chapters that you need in this book. Develop your psychological strengths. Plan your strategy. You will find that you have become your own "mental coach," able to bring out the best in your game.

You may even find that goal setting and imagery are useful skills for other areas of your life. That's a nice bonus. Now put the book down and go out there and have fun!

INDEX

❑YES, I want _____ copies of *Sport Psychology Library: Tennis* at $12.95 each, plus $3.00 shipping and only $1.00 shipping for each additional book ordered. All orders are payable in U.S. dollars.

(West Virginia residents please add 6% sales tax)

❑My check or money order is enclosed.

Please make your check payable and return to:

Fitness Information Technology, Inc.
P. O. Box 4425
Morgantown, WV 26504-4425

❑Please charge to my VISA, MasterCard, or American Express card. See below or . . .

Call toll free at 800-477-4348

Or You Can Order by:
Phone/Fax: 304-599-3482
Email: fit@fitinfotech.com
Website: www.fitinfotech.com

Give this Unique
Book as a

GIFT
TO
FRIENDS
AND
FAMILY

*CHECK
YOUR
FAVORITE
BOOKSTORE
OR ORDER
HERE*

Bill To:

Name _____

Address _____

_____

_____

_____

Phone _____

Email _____

Card # _____

Exp. Date _____

Signature _____

Ship To (if different)

Name _____

Address _____

_____

_____

_____

Phone _____

Email _____

❑ YES, I want _____ copies of *Sport Psychology Library: Tennis* at $12.95 each, plus $3.00 shipping and only $1.00 shipping for each additional book ordered. All orders are payable in U.S. dollars.

(West Virginia residents please add 6% sales tax)

❑ My check or money order is enclosed.

Please make your check payable and return to:

Fitness Information Technology, Inc.
P. O. Box 4425
Morgantown, WV 26504-4425

❑ Please charge to my VISA, MasterCard, or American Express card. See below or . . .

Call toll free at 800-477-4348

Or You Can Order by:
Phone/Fax: 304-599-3482
Email: fit@fitinfotech.com
Website: www.fitinfotech.com

Give this Unique Book as a

GIFT
TO
FRIENDS
AND
FAMILY

CHECK
YOUR
FAVORITE
BOOKSTORE
OR ORDER
HERE

Bill To:

Name _____

Address _____

_____

_____

_____

Phone _____

Email _____

Card # _____

Exp. Date _____

Signature _____

Ship To (if different)

Name _____

Address _____

_____

_____

_____

Phone _____

Email _____

❑YES, I want _____ copies of *Sport Psychology Library: Tennis* at $12.95 each, plus $3.00 shipping and only $1.00 shipping for each additional book ordered. All orders are payable in U.S. dollars.

(West Virginia residents please add 6% sales tax)

❑My check or money order is enclosed.

Please make your check payable and return to:

Fitness Information Technology, Inc.
P. O. Box 4425
Morgantown, WV 26504-4425

❑Please charge to my VISA, MasterCard, or American Express card. See below or . . .

Call toll free at 800-477-4348

Or You Can Order by:
Phone/Fax: 304-599-3482
Email: fit@fitinfotech.com
Website: www.fitinfotech.com

Give this Unique
Book as a

GIFT
TO
FRIENDS
AND
FAMILY

CHECK
YOUR
FAVORITE
BOOKSTORE
OR ORDER
HERE

Bill To:

Name _____

Address _____

_____

_____

_____

Phone _____

Email _____

Card # _____

Exp. Date _____

Signature _____

Ship To (if different)

Name _____

Address _____

_____

_____

_____

Phone _____

Email _____